Praise for
Damn! That's Funny!
and Gene Perret

The late comedian Bob Hope once said of Gene Perret...

"You know, I travel a lot—all over the world—and when I need some extra-special material, I call Gene Perret. ...Gene teaches that a sense of humor should be a big part of our lives. I've certainly found that to be true."

— *Bob Hope*

"[Gene Perret] was instrumental in starting me down the road to where I am today. In fact, I can say for certain that I wouldn't even be in show business if it weren't for the things I learned from Gene. Now, I can't say for certain that if you read Gene's book you'll have the same good fortune as I've had. But if you don't read it, you'll never know."

— *Joe Medeiros, head writer, "The Tonight Show with Jay Leno"*

"Gene Perret, the world's top authority on comedy writing, comedy thinking, comedy presentation, has written the definitive book to teach you how to make your writing sing."

— *Phyllis Diller*

"Gene Perret has an incredible mind! He's one of the top five comedy writers in the world. Whatever he tells you in this book, listen to him. He's right!"

— *Arnie Kogen, television and film writer, winner of three Emmy awards*

"Gene is brilliant, provocative, and very attractive."

— *Harvey Korman*

DAMN!

THAT'S FUNNY!

Writing Humor You Can Sell

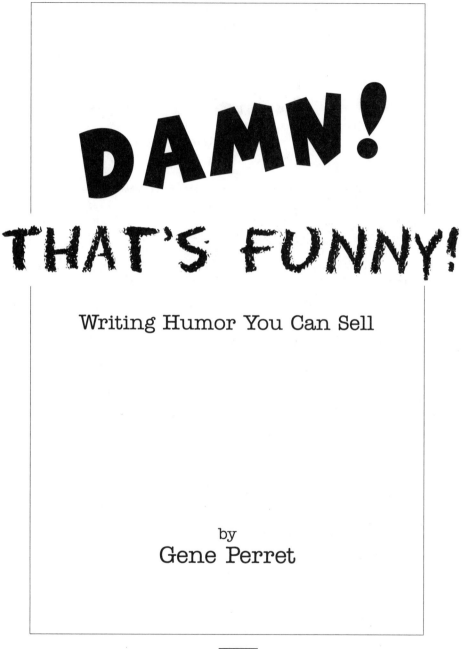

DAMN!
THAT'S FUNNY!

Writing Humor You Can Sell

by
Gene Perret

Quill
Driver
Books

Sanger, California

Published by Quill Driver Books/Word Dancer Press, Inc.
1254 Commerce Blvd.
Sanger, California 93657
559-876-2170 • 1-800-497-4909 • FAX 559-876-2180
QuillDriverBooks.com
Info@QuillDriverBooks.com

Quill Driver Books' titles may be purchased in quantity at special discounts for educational, fund-raising, business, or promotional use. Please contact Special Markets, Quill Driver Books/Word Dancer Press, Inc. at the above address or at **1-800-497-4909**.

Quill Driver Books/Word Dancer Press, Inc. project cadre:
Kathy Chillemi, Doris Hall, Linda Kay Hardie, Stephen Blake Mettee, Manya Slevkoff

ISBN: 1-884956-44-0

Printed in the United States of America

QUILL DRIVER BOOKS and colophon are trademarks of Quill Driver Books/Word Dancer Press, Inc.

To order another copy of this book, please call
1-800-497-4909

Library of Congress Cataloging-in-Publication Data

Perret, Gene.
Damn! that's funny! : the professional guide to writing humorous articles you can sell.
p. cm.
Includes bibliographical references and index.
ISBN 1-884956-44-0 (trade paper-back : alk. paper)
1. Wit and humor--Authorship. I. Title.
PN6149.A88P463 2005
808.7--dc22

2005008250

In memory of
a legendary humorist,
Bob Hope

ontents

Foreword

The casual observer may think that learning to write humor is just for those who want to create amusing newspaper or magazine columns, sitcom scripts, jokes, gag lines for comic strips and the like.

Professional authors know, however, that the techniques of creating humor benefit all writers, even if they have no intention of ever writing a joke. Like untold hundreds of others, I have learned that from Gene Perret, a master of comedy writing.

Learning to write humor will—and I emphasize will—make you a better observer, and better observation will make whatever you write stronger and more compelling. You'll notice details in scenes that have escaped your attention, mannerisms that you never heeded, subtle attitudes that belie a person's deeper motives that heretofore passed you by. For example, take the case of Charlie, who refers to himself as "we" instead of "I." That's a mannerism everyone eventually notices. But a better observer will discover why he does that—because he is introverted and unsure of himself—and these kinds of details add drama and impact to any piece of writing.

Learning to write humor will force you to examine situations in unconventional, sometimes even bizarre ways. Such examination leads to insight, the highest goal of any communication. Comedy writers depend heavily on insight. It helps them discover the punch line, the surprise ending. But all writers strive for insight, insight into a character's attitudes, insight into a person's motivations, insight into current events, especially those that are complex and difficult to understand. Television shows make a lot of money on the segments of their newscasts that attempt to provide insight into weather patterns. We watch because we not only want to know what the weather will be tomorrow, but why. Learning to write humor will help expand your vocabulary. If you try to tell a joke and use the wrong word—maybe even a word that is close to but not exactly on point—no one will laugh. Humor writing teaches the precise use of the language, and all writers—comedy or otherwise—benefit from precision.

Learning to write humor will help you write concisely, another attribute that benefits all writers. Wordiness is the death knell of humor, especially for punch lines. Each sentence of a piece of humor must be crisp and concise; otherwise it loses its effect and no one laughs, a type of immediate feedback. Wordiness in other types of prose simply evokes boredom, causing the reader to lose concentration and, therefore, interest. But there is no instant feedback, and so the writer may never know he's failed. Comedy writing provides that instant response and thus helps a writer hone his craft.

Knowing and using the techniques of humor writing will improve any form of writing. In fact, I believe that learning the techniques of humor writing will improve your writing quicker than any other method I know of.

I have known and worked with Gene Perret for about ten years. He writes a very popular column for *Arizona Highways* magazine and for the magazine's web site. His columns are always insightful and always funny, often laugh-out-loud funny. I have read Gene's books, attended his workshops and studied his humor-writing methods.

I've learned his techniques so well that I've taught them for years in a writing class at Arizona State University West. And I can attest that Gene's methods work. Always in the first session of the semester a few students write jokes that cause everyone to laugh. By the second class all the students are writing jokes that draw laughter. And when we move on to other topics, such as dialogue and characterization, humor consistently creeps into that writing also. Students love it. And so will you once you've absorbed Gene's comedy-writing methods.

Bob Early, Editor
Arizona Highways

PART I

Preparing to Write Humor

Chapter One

The Positive Side of Writing Humor (and a few non-positives)

When British actor Edmund Keane was on his death bed, a comforting friend said, "This must be very difficult for you." Keane replied, "Dying is easy. Comedy is difficult."

It's probably indelicate to quarrel with a man's dying words, but Eddie was wrong. Well, maybe he was inaccurate rather than incorrect. Since he wasn't feeling himself that day, we'll give him the benefit of the doubt. Humor is more intimidating than it is difficult.

It's like speaking before an audience. Some survey taken a few years ago listed the fear of speaking in public more potent than the fear of dying. People admitted that they would rather jump into their death bed than be required to deliver a speech. Yet, speaking in public is not difficult. A person who can speak can speak in public simply by getting in front of a public and speaking. It's that simple.

But some can't do it. I once asked a friend of mine whom I had guided into the comedy writing field to address a seminar I was holding for aspiring comedy writers. This gentleman said, "Gene, I owe you a lot. I will wash and iron your shirts for you. I will mow your lawn biweekly. I just can't stand in front of a group of people and speak."

People are intimidated by speaking and by humor. They're afraid they'll do badly. Consequently people surrender. "I can't do humor," people say. At the comedy writing seminars that I used to conduct annually, I encouraged aspiring writers to try to deliver their own comedy. It was a way of appreciating good comedy writing. If a person did well, she realized how valuable good comedy writing was. If a person did badly, he realized how damaging weak comedy material could be. It generated a genuine appreciation for the craft of comedy writing. One writer, though, actually said, "If I stand up there and try to tell jokes, people will laugh at me."

By dismissing this form of writing, many of us are missing out on a good thing. Humor is fun. It's fun to write. As you write, you also become part of your own audience and when you get off a *good one*, you enjoy it as much as your readers will when they see it in print. Maybe more.

I enjoy writing humor. I've been doing it for most of my adult life, although it is a stretch to call a comedy writer "adult." Finding the humor in everyday situations is fun. It's also fun to put it on paper and to see it in print. I must confess that when I read my column each month when *Arizona Highways* arrives, I chuckle and invariably say, "I'm a funny guy."

> "Finding the humor in everyday situations is fun. It's also fun to put it on paper and to see it in print."

The response is a kick, too. It's always nice to get a compliment about anything you write, but somehow the accolades about the humorous articles always seem more enthusiastic. "I read your article about the way that they measure the tolerances in manufacturing airplane parts. It was interesting." That's nice to hear. "Hey, I read the article about your brother. My wife and I laughed ourselves silly." That's nicer to hear. Of course, I haven't heard from my brother yet about that article, but...

People enjoy humor. Each month *Reader's Digest* surveys their readers and the humor departments usually finish at the top of the list. You probably do what I do, and what most readers do. You pick up the *Digest*, look at the table of contents, and then leaf through the magazine for the joke pages and the fillers. After that, you read the articles you're interested in. I'm always amazed at the reaction of readers to some articles and columns that I think are a bit weak. People still say they enjoyed them. Readers love to be entertained and they're willing to accept some of the lesser articles along with the occasional brilliant ones. I know from my experience with performers that they love to hear the applause. Well, we writers like to hear "applause" once in a while, too.

Writing humor can be cathartic. If some clown cuts you off while you're driving along the highway, write a blisteringly funny article about clowns who drive like that. If an old lady jumps ahead of you at the supermarket check-out counter, she's going to be the star of one of your upcoming comedic pieces. She may never read it, but you will have written it. That's revenge enough.

Trash the query letters

Like most writers, I'm a tad on the lazy side. Most of us prefer opening envelopes with a check in them to stuffing envelopes with material we've written. Once a partner and I submitted a project and got a very enthusiastic letter of acceptance in return. I tried to celebrate, but my partner was glum. I asked what the problem was since we had just made a sale with a generous advance. He said, "Yeah, but now we have to write the damn thing."

Since we are that kind of animal, I like the fact that no query letters are required with humorous article writing. They're not only not required, but they serve no purpose. Suppose you're an editor and you get a query letter asking if you'd like to see an 850-word piece about returning a bottle of wine in a restaurant. Would you buy it? Do you want it? You have no way of knowing. The value of humor is in the execution, not necessarily in the premise.

When I go to the dentist I return with sore jowls and wanting nothing more chewable than noodle soup for a day or two. Bill Cosby returns from the dentist with a hilarious routine about rinsing, and a mouth full of cotton, and gums numbed with Novocain.

Besides, most humorous articles are relatively short—about 750 to 850 words. You can write the entire article in the time it would take you to compose a quality query letter. So write the piece and send it out. Then the editor will know whether your treatment of this topic is funny or not.

Since you don't send a query letter, you can't have an editor reject your idea. Consequently, you can write about anything you want to write about. That's delicious freedom for a writer. You want to write about the rude teller at your bank, have at it. Are you upset because your wife keeps switching over to a cooking show while you're trying to watch a football game and take a nap at the same time? Start banging those keys. You may not sell every piece, but so what? You had fun writing them.

A writing colleague of mine once sold a concept to *Reader's Digest*. It's a prestigious periodical and they pay well, so he was delighted. He sent in his first draft of a 1,500-word article. In return he got a 7,000-word critique of his 1,500-word first draft. He still had the sale, but he had a lot more research to do, many more interviews to conduct, and lots of retyping before his words made it into print.

> **"You may not sell every piece, but so what? You had fun writing them."**

As a humor writer, I relish avoiding all that sort of work. Some writers dote on it. They love to hit the library, research on the Internet, and arrange live interviews with folks connected to their article. Fine. Let them do it. I'd much prefer to do no research, conduct no interviews, and simply rip into that old biddy who pushed ahead of me at the supermarket.

Not all chuckles and applause

From a practical point of view, though, the real plus of humor writing is that there is a genuine demand for it. When I lectured at several colleges with *Reader's Digest* I listened to the presentations of many high level editors from the nation's top periodicals. Most of them said in essence that they wanted humor—they needed humor. Yet, at the same time, they said that they had trouble finding good humorists. For a writer, this is the ideal situation—a market that needs material and not too many competitors who will supply it.

So it is an inviting market, but there is a downside, also. That's right—writing humor is not all chuckles and applause. There are some non-positives. Humor can be a tough sell. One editor told me that when she received a humorous piece that caused her to laugh out loud, she'd pass it on to another editor. He, too, would roar at it. Then it would go to the next one, and so on down the line. This editor told me that if six of them fell on the floor laughing, and one was on the fence about it, they'd reject it.

Remember we said that humor is more intimidating than it is difficult. Well, it intimidates editors as well as writers.

Editors claim they can't find good humorists, but some of that trouble in finding good humorists lies with the editors rather than with the humorists. Humor can intimidate the buyers as well as the sellers. Many of the editors are afraid to say, "Yes, this is a funny piece of writing." It's too much of a commitment for them.

However, there is a positive side even to this non-positive. Once you break through this editorial barrier, you carry much more weight with those editors. With almost every humorous article I've sold, the publication asked for additional articles. They're afraid of humor so when they find a humorist they can trust, they lean on that person.

Another non-positive is that many editors don't know comedy. They're good at what they do, but humor is a foreign language to many of them. Sometimes their demands can suck any of the fun out of a piece. The best example I can offer wasn't from a periodical but on a television show. Phyllis Diller years ago guested on Ed Sullivan's show. Sullivan needed to cut back on time, so he picked on Phyllis's act. He reviewed her script and asked her to cut out half of the lines because, in his words, "They weren't funny." However, those lines were the set-up lines. They were the words that made the punch lines funny. Without them, Phyllis had gibberish.

Diller opted out of the show rather than do the lines the way Ed Sullivan wanted them done.

Another non-positive in writing humor is that it can often be dangerous. Comedy usually has a "victim." The funny lines mock or ridicule someone or something. That's basically what humor is. Someone once observed that he didn't think there would be humor in heaven because everyone there would be perfect and with total perfection you have nothing to belittle. That's a bit too philosophical for me, but maybe by this time, the British actor Edmund Keane knows whether that's true or not.

Nonetheless, you do kid someone and some editors are afraid of that. I know the editor of a religious magazine told me that they avoided humor at all costs. Why? Because people invariably thought it was sacrilegious.

It is true, too, that even good-natured humor can look cruel in print. Often you get a letter with a snippy remark in it and you wonder were they kidding or did they really mean it.

As a writer, you can protect yourself by being very aware of what you write. Read it as your reader might perceive it. Try to keep an even-handed humor in your writing. Someone once asked Will Rogers how he managed to kid the most powerful men in the world without getting into trouble. Rogers said, "If there's no malice in your heart, then there can't be none in your jokes." It's worthwhile advice.

Another gambit is to make yourself the victim. No one is going to take offense if you come down a little hard on yourself.

Chapter Two

What Does It Take to Write Humor?

A gag-writer friend of mine visited a foot specialist regularly to care for his aching "piggies." He was an outgoing character and he and the Doc became good buddies. During one examination he asked the doctor, "Why did you ever decide to adopt such an unglamorous medical specialty—dealing with feet all day?" The doctor defended his choice. He said, "The foot is an intriguing part of the human anatomy. There are twenty-six bones in the foot, which is one-fourth of all the bones in the entire body. There are thirty-three joints, over one hundred muscles, tendons, and ligaments, and there is a vast network of blood vessels, soft tissue, skin, and nerves. It's fascinating detective work to find out what causes problems in the foot area."

My friend said, "Baloney."

The Doc said, "Baloney?"

My pal said, "You just got to medical school and found out that it was really hard so you said, 'I think I'll just quit once I get up to the ankle.'"

No. The specialist has to be a doctor first. A humor writer is a specialist, but a writer nonetheless. You must sharpen your skills by reading good writing, studying, and, of course, writing. Someone once said that there are only three ways to learn to write—write, write, and write.

To put together a funny sentence, you must know how to construct a sentence. To tell a humorous story, you must be a story teller. Whatever it takes to become a good writer is the foundation for becoming a good humor writer. However, there are certain skills you should develop to become a specialist—a humor writer.

Observation:

Often, humor is pointing out the obvious—the obvious that most people rarely notice. Wait. Isn't that contradictory? If something is obvious, wouldn't everybody notice it? Not necessarily.

Do this experiment with me. Place your right hand over your watch. If you're left-handed, place your left hand over your watch. If you're wearing two watches, just put your hands behind your back or call a friend to help you with this test. Now that your watch (or watches) is/are safely out of view, tell me what the numeral six looks like on your watch. Also, tell me how the hands on your watch are shaped. Are they straight? Curved? Do they have an arrowhead-like thing at the end?

Give it a good effort and try to recall what these things look like. Now look at your watch. You were probably wrong if you hazarded a guess at all. Right? You look at your watch several times a day. The number six (if there is one) and the hands are in plain view. In order to tell time, you have to see them…but you never really do see them. They're obvious, but you never notice them.

Comedian David Brenner had a great example of the obvious in his act. He talked about the Superman movies where some thug would fire his gun repeatedly at Superman. The hero would put his hands on his hips and thrust his chest out, acting a bit smug as the bullets bounced harmlessly off his chest. Then when the gun was emptied, the gangster would hurl it at Superman. And what did Superman do? He ducked. He scoffed at the bullets, but flinched when the gun came toward him.

I had watched a variation of that scene countless times, but never realized it was funny until David Brenner highlighted it for me.

George Carlin thought it was funny that we would *park* in *driveways*, but *drive* on *parkways*. I knew that, but never appreciated the irony of it until George Carlin made a point of it.

Both of these ideas were there. They were obvious. It took a humorist to point them out.

There's a wealth of such phenomena in our culture. But how do we, as humorists, uncover them? We do it by developing the power of our observation. Most of us see only what we need to see. As our experiment showed, we look at our watch often but see only what we want to see. We see what time it is and little else.

You probably can't recall where the fuel gauge is on the dashboard of your car. Is it to the right or left of the speedometer? Is it towards the top of the control panel or the bottom? You must look at that periodically, but you don't really see it.

I once worked on a television show with a writer who had a full beard. Many of us ate at the same restaurant each day, including this writer, and we usually had the same waitress. After about three months, this writer shaved his beard. He left the moustache, but got rid of the beard. When we went to lunch, we asked the waitress, "Do you notice anything different about Harry?" She looked and looked, but couldn't notice anything different. Finally, her eyes brightened and she said, "Oh yeah. You grew a moustache."

How can we learn to find the obvious that people usually overlook? How can we discover these ironies? The answer is by looking for them. It's part of our duties as humorists. Once we start looking for them with purpose, many of them become easier to spot.

David Brenner discovered the hilarious inconsistency in Superman's reactions because he went looking for it. He went searching for something and found that. Carlin saw the humor in parking in driveways and driving on parkways because he searched for it. He was researching the fun in words, and uncovered these.

On TV detective shows, we learn that the ace detectives always see things at the crime scene that ordinary folks overlook. It's part of their training and a result of their experience. That's what we humor writers should train ourselves to do also. Learn to observe and see things. The more you notice about our world, the more humor you'll find in it.

Be aware of what you see, too. As I mentioned earlier, I can come home from a visit to the dentist with nothing but an aching jaw and some tender gums. Bill Cosby comes home with eight minutes of hilarity for his audience. Why? Because he filters everything through his comedic eye.

I worked with a standup comedian one time and he was in a serious accident. His car flipped over and he was lying in the wreckage, temporarily paralyzed. He admitted that he honestly didn't know if he was alive or dead. But he did remember what he thought about as he waited for help to arrive. He thought to himself, "What's funny about this?"

Now that's devotion to one's craft.

Analyzation:

Here's an interesting challenge for potential humor writers: try to come up with a humorous observation about Mother's Day, and only Mother's Day. It's impossible. You can't do it. Surely, some magazines would like a short, humorous piece in May that features Mother's Day. You know you are a funny writer. However, I guarantee you that you cannot come up with one funny observation about that holiday, and only that holiday.

Now I've come across some funny bits in pieces about Moms on their special day.

One humorist noted:

I told my Mom on Mother's Day, "Mom, you've been bending over a hot stove all your life. Straighten up."

Another observed:

Mother's Day always falls on a Sunday in May, shortly after March, which is National Peanut Butter Month. What kind of people are we? We devote one day to the woman who gave us life and an entire month to a jar of peanut butter.

One author wrote:

For Mother's Day, the kids and I served their Mom breakfast in bed. She was surprised and thrilled. Of course, it took her until four o'clock in the afternoon to clean up the kitchen.

They're all funny concepts. Aren't they about Mother's Day? No, not really. They're all about Mother's Day in connection with something else. One is about a particular Mom who bends over a stove. Another relates Mother's Day to peanut butter. The last is about just one aspect of that day—serving the honoree breakfast in bed.

None of them are about Mother's Day, and only that day. I still maintain that's an impossibility.

The point I'm trying to illustrate is that in order to generate humor about any subject, you must dissect that subject. You must pull it apart and discover its hidden facets. Find out what makes it interesting, what makes it unique. In fact, find out all you can about your premise. The more you uncover about your subject, the more fun you'll be able to find in it. Maybe more important, the humor you do create will be more incisive because you will have uncovered areas that are more unique.

The harder you investigate your subject, the better chance you have of discovering those ironies that we talked about earlier—those obvious facts that everyone seems to have missed. That's when you create solid humor—when you come up with ideas that everyone is thinking about, but no one has thought of.

Analyzing your premise is an important part of all humor writing. Before you can be funny, you must give yourself something to be funny about. Mother's Day is a fine premise, but it's not enough. You have to combine that subject with other ideas. How do you do that?

Let's stay with the concept of Mother's Day for this experiment and see how to analyze a topic for humor.

The first step is some basic research. I just got on the internet and discovered that there was a form of Mother's Day celebrated in Ancient Greece. President Woodrow Wilson declared the second Sunday in May a national holiday honoring mothers. In the United States, it was first promoted in 1872 by Julia Ward Howe who wrote the words to "The Battle Hymn of the Republic." There may be other interesting historical facts about the holidays that you can uncover.

Will any of these items lead to humorous concepts for your article? I don't know, and you probably don't either, but having them available gives you ammunition for possible funny ideas.

Next, make a personal list of anything related to your own Mother's Day observances. The items don't have to be funny. They're simply fodder for the fun you can have with them. The more items you can uncover, the more information you'll have to work with.

Why not take a moment right now and try to create such a list.

Let me offer my own example:

I was asked to write a humor piece for *McCall's* magazine's May issue on this very topic. At that time, the last page of *McCall's* magazine was devoted to humor. It was called "To Leave You Laughing... ." This page had several aphorisms and a few cartoons on one particular topic.

My slant was to do some humorous one-liners about how much my Mom loved me...in spite of me and my behavior. My list of concepts included that my mother loved me even when I got in trouble at school...I fought with my siblings...I kept her awake as a cranky baby...I got in with a bad crowd...I broke her valuables...I lost her valuables...I had to be punished...I was costing her money...and I'm sure many others.

From that list I offered the following eighteen lines to the editors. Typically, this page published only about seven to ten lines, but I always liked to offer more so that they could select the ones they wanted to use.

Here's the manuscript I submitted. The gags they used in their May 1987 issue are marked.

1) **Mom, you got this special day the hard way—you earned it. (This was a play on a popular TV commercial of the time.** *McCall's* **used it as the sub-title for the feature.)**

2) **You loved me when I got my days and nights mixed up. That was when I was a newborn infant and also during my senior and junior years in high school. (used)**

3) **You loved me through what you called "the five toughest years of your life"—when I was two years old. (used)**

4) **You loved me when I lost things you cherished—like my little brother who disappeared for two hours at the Church Picnic. (used)**

5) **You loved me when I fought with my brothers and sisters. For the record, though, Mom, they always started the fights by hitting me back.**

6) **You loved me when you were called to the high school after my first semester. It was the first time the teacher had met you...and me, too, for that matter.**

7) **You loved me when I played my music so loud that the neighbors called to complain—for two years after they moved away.**

8) You loved me even after the first time I ran away from home. You did know I couldn't get too far because I wasn't allowed to cross the streets yet.

9) You loved me when I made you angrier than words can describe, although the words you used generally got the idea across. (used)

10) You loved me through all the phases I went through and even a couple that you went through because of the ones I went through.

11) You loved me enough to teach me wrong from right. Sometimes I couldn't sit down for a while after the lessons.

12) You didn't always punish me when I was naughty. Sometimes you let Dad have his fun, too.

13) You loved me even when my room was a mess, which covers all of my life and a goodly portion of yours.

14) You loved me even those times when we didn't see eye to eye. Of course, it's hard for me to see eye to eye with a person when I'm bent over their knee.

15) You even loved some of the friends I brought over to the house—once you figured out what they were. (used)

16) You loved me even during those times when no one else would, could, or should.

17) I love you because you carried me before my birth for nine long months; and in college, you carried me for four long years.

I think you can see that even though this is a humor piece on Mother's Day, it covers a broad range of topics. All of them, though, are related to the main premise. That's why you want to analyze and dissect your topic and generate as much information as you can about it before you start your humorous writing.

Another reason for analyzing your topic is because most humor is comparison. Take a look at some of your favorite one-liners and you'll notice that almost all of them are comparisons or are relating one concept to another. That's why I suggested earlier that it's practically impossible to come up with a funny concept about Mother's Day, and only Mother's Day. There's nothing to compare it with or relate it to, so it's just sitting there in a vacuum.

To create humor, we almost always have to compare one topic to another. Discovering what's similar or what's different about two ideas, helps in formulating funny concepts.

For instance, the breakfast in bed concept is very much related to Mother's Day. So that line about serving Mom her morning meal in bed and then her working until four in the afternoon to clean the kitchen is appropriate.

However, Father's Day could be considered the opposite of Mother's Day, so that can be used, too. As an example:

I'm sorry, but there is more love attached to Mother's Day than there is to Father's Day. On her special day, the kids served their Mom breakfast in bed. On my special day, they came close. They let me sleep in the kitchen.

Again, I recommend making a list of topics, ideas, names, places, sayings that are related to your main topic, either by being similar to it or noticeably different from it.

Irreverence

Another quality that's helpful to a humor writer is a sense of irreverence. I don't mean that in the vicious sense of the word. I'm not promoting destroying traditions that are held dear and sacred. I do mean refusing to accept the seriousness of any situation. By being irreverent, I mean you purposely look for the fun rather than the gravity in everything.

"Whimsy" is a word that I considered to describe this attitude, but it seemed too genteel a word, too kind, too generous. Whimsy, to me, implies finding fun in situations that are already fun. It's like finding fun at a party. That's easy. Anyone can do that. A humorous writer should be able to find fun in being hopelessly stuck in traffic on the way home from a grueling day at the office.

Earlier I told you about a humorist friend of mine who was in a serious accident. While he was in his overturned car, unable to move, not knowing whether he would survive the event or not, he thought, "What's funny about this?" That's the ultimate of the irreverent attitude you should be developing.

Condition yourself to go for the wackiness in any circumstances rather than for the gravity or the reality. This doesn't connote being inconsiderate. It's simply training yourself to see the comedy in the world around you.

As a humor writer, train yourself to see the unusual, the bizarre, the zany, the wacky, the funny in whatever you observe. Don't allow reality and pomposity to obscure your humorous point of view.

Dave Barry's humor writing is a fine example of this attitude. His writing is funny and irreverent. He'll often lead the reader to believe he's making a serious point, then he'll hit the reader with an off-the-wall, outlandish, bizarre, funny conclusion. It's a great skill for a humorist.

I've worked with great humor writers for most of my career. Several of them perfected this skill to the point where they rarely would give a normal response in any conversation. They developed the ability to convert even the most ordinary of questions to a straight line.

Once I traveled to Tahiti for a television special. During some free time, I headed to the beach for some sun and a swim in the ocean. On my way, I met another writer who was returning from the beach. "How's the water?" I asked. He said, "Needs more salt."

I had dinner once with a comedy writer who used to work for George Burns, who at that time was in his nineties. This writer was now writing for Bob Hope, who at that time was in his eighties. During dinner I asked why he had switched from Burns to Hope. He said, "I wanted to get with a younger comedian."

Bob Hope himself was the epitome of this irreverent attitude. He looked for the humor in everything. On his seventieth birthday, I knew Hope well enough to ask him, "Can you still have sex at seventy?" Hope replied, "Sure, but I think it's safer to pull over to the side of the road."

This is the sort of irreverence that you should develop. You may not make it your lifestyle, as some of my comedy writing friends did, but it certainly should become part of your humor writing arsenal.

Chapter Three

What Makes a Good Humorous Article Idea?

Producers, head-writers, and veteran writers experienced in television situation comedies make a pronouncement that fledgling sitcom writers often question or reject outright. That statement is that the most important element in a good situation comedy script is the structure. "No," young writers object, "the jokes are paramount." Their thinking is that these are comedy shows. Comedy requires jokes. Consequently, the gags are the most significant factor of any script.

Laughs are essential to a comedy show. However, many inexperienced writers begin a project by assembling a collection of hilarious lines, and then they try to string those lines into a series of incidents. The result is a weak plot. It's disjointed and lacks credibility.

When one creates a strong premise and works it into a believable, well-structured plot, it gives the characters in the play something to *joke* about. Now their quips, their barbs, their insults are part of the story. Now they add to the tale that's being told rather than distracting from it.

Funny characters, too, are necessary. Nevertheless, the characters need something to do. They must be placed into intriguing predicaments. Only then can they be funny. Archie Bunker was a powerful comedy figure in television sitcoms. If Archie Bunker just sat in his famous easy chair watching television and asking Edith "What's for dinner?" the show would never have become a TV classic.

The same principle obtains in writing a good humorous article. It needs a solid premise to generate the whimsy. Certainly you want to be funny, but you want to be funny *about something*. That something is your premise.

What then are the elements that constitute a good premise on which to start writing a humorous piece? I'll list two and then add a third which should be employed whenever possible.

1) The idea should be true.

2) The idea should be recognizable.

3) Whenever possible, the idea should be localized.

Let's take a look at each of these.

1) The idea should be true:

Comedy must be based on truth. Read and listen to some of these one-liners from great stand-up comedians:

"Life begins at forty, but so does arthritis and the habit of telling the same story three times to the same person."
—**Jack E. Leonard**

"We usually meet all our relatives only at funerals where someone always observes, 'It's too bad we can't get together like this more often.'"
—**Sam Levenson**

"I once went on a three-week diet and lost twenty-one days."
—**Henny Youngman**

"Health nuts are going to feel real stupid one day—lying in hospitals dying of nothing."
—**Redd Foxx**

"The only way to solve the traffic problem is to pass a law that only cars that are paid for are allowed on the highways."
—**Will Rogers**

These are all funny lines from funny people, but you notice that each of them has an element of truth connected to it. In fact, it's basically the truth that gets us laughing. Oh sure, the humorist has to couch that truth in an original, clever, inventive way. That enhances the comedy value, but it needs to start with a truth.

A humorous piece, too, should be based on truth. That truth can be exaggerated, distorted, twisted, convoluted, or stretched to its extremes. Following are a couple of articles showing how truth is an essential element in humor. Throughout this book, I'll try to include samples of the principles discussed. Often, seeing the technique in print is more illuminating than simply discussing the theory. Also, I feel it gives you a model to guide your own writing.

This first article is based purely on truth—that business firms now have automated telephone systems that are infuriating to us customers. The second article shows how truth can be toyed with. The piece is about me having to deal with some noisy neighbors. That was true. The distortion, though, is that these particular noisy neighbors usually don't talk. You'll see what I mean when you read it.

Hello! You're Speaking to Absolutely No One

The telephone used to be a delightful form of communication. You'd call to see how people were feeling, to find out how the kids were doing in school, just to say "hello." Remember the phrase, "Gee, it's good to hear your voice"? It doesn't apply anymore. You no longer hear a voice; you hear a machine.

With today's technology they have a machine that can dial your machine. These two androids converse. Their machine tells your machine when it can call back their machine. They even have machines that can check the number of your machine and if they don't like the number of your machine, they won't even let you talk to their machine. No humans are required.

If the world ended tomorrow, the telephone companies would continue to make money for the next three, maybe four, months.

The telephone, which used to be fun, has become frustrating.

A while ago I ordered some merchandise through a mail order catalog. Last week the shipment arrived. It was the wrong color, wrong model number, wrong size, wrong price, and batteries were supposed to be included, but weren't. Of course, the merchandise was guaranteed. "If our merchandise fails to meet your satisfaction for any reason..." Another two and a half paragraphs of unconditional guaranteeing ended with the words, "Simply call our customer service department."

I called. The phone rang twenty-eight times which didn't really meet my satisfaction, either.

Finally, a voice said, "Hello."

I said, "Good morning," but the voice at the other end ignored my greeting and went on. I had just offered a good morning to a weird, mechanical voice that sounded like it could use a good, long gargle with 3-in-1 oil.

The voice said, "Your call is very important to us."

"Then why didn't you hire a real person to answer it?" I said that to myself because whatever was at the other end of the phone line wasn't listening to me.

"All of our operators are busy at the moment," the voice politely explained, assuming that machines can be polite. "But if you'll please stay on the line, the calls will be answered in the order in which they were received."

I quickly said, "But I want to..." I didn't say it quickly enough. The phone clicked and I was listening to music. The music was soothing and pleasant. If I closed my eyes I almost felt like I was riding in an elevator.

The problem was I didn't want to ride an elevator, I wanted to get the merchandise I ordered and paid for.

After a brief wait of about seven weeks, the phone clicked again and another eerie voice said, "If you wish to continue in English, press one." I pressed one and another robotic voice talked to me in Spanish? German? Lithuanian? Swahili? I don't know which language. It wasn't English; I knew that much. Their telephone system must have been set up by the same person who packed my order.

I hung up and dialed again. All their operators were still busy. They were probably off studying a foreign language at Berlitz. When I finally got the menu, I tried pressing one again and this time got an English speaking automatonic voice. It said, "If you wish to place an order, press one. If you wish to inquire about the status of an order not yet received, press two. If you wish information about other merchandise, press three. Press now."

"Press now?" None of those are the reason I called. I hung up and dialed again.

I heard the same complaint about how busy their operators were, the same elevator music, and the same phone menu. I outsmarted them. I pressed 0 for operator.

It worked. I got another mechanical voice. It said, "Please enter your customer number which is in the yellow box on the mailing label on your shipping cartoon." The carton was in the garage. I set the phone down and raced out to find the box the wrong merchandise arrived in.

When I got back to the phone, all I heard was a dial tone.

I remembered when I called to place the order I spoke with a live operator who gladly accepted my credit card number and expiration date. Aha, I thought, that's my revenge.

I dialed the "place an order" number. A real person answered quickly. "Would you like to place an order?" she asked.

"Yes I would," I said. "I'd like to spend a lot of money with your company."

"Wonderful," she said, "And what can we send you from our catalog?"

I said, "If you think I want to order something from pages one to twenty-five, press one. If you think I want to order something from pages twenty-six to fifty, press two..."

She hung up and I smirked.

Here's the article that stretches the truth a bit:

Neighborly Disagreement

My wife and I recently moved into a new home. It's a modestly sized home, but large enough for each of us to have our privacy. The neighborhood is clean, safe, and the people in the community are friendly. Our property is small, but the house is nestled up against the foothills so from our back yard we enjoy a beautiful panorama of shrubbery and brush, quail and roadrunners darting around. It's the ideal home.

Well, it's almost the ideal home. We have some noisy neighbors. They're noisy at the most annoying hours—sometimes at one or two o'clock in the morning.

The other morning, at about two A.M., their clamor woke my wife and almost woke me. "This is ridiculous," she said.

I mumbled something and rolled over.

"It's got to stop," she said.

I mumbled again and rolled back to where I was before.

"Go talk to them," she said.

I said, "It's two o'clock in the morning."

"That's why you have to talk to them. People are supposed to sleep at this time."

"I'll talk to them tomorrow."

"Now," she said. "Tomorrow we'll forget about it, we'll be forgiving. Talk to them now."

I got up, threw on a shirt and slacks, slipped into my shoes— one should be dressed properly to go raise hell with the neighbors about the hell they're raising—and marched up the hill.

There they were, the whole family, openly and boldly yipping, yapping, yelping, barking, howling. You see, they were a family of coyotes.

I said to them, "Yo…hey folks. What do you say you hold it down a bit? You know there are people around here who are trying to sleep."

One of them, I suppose the head of the household, said, "What's your problem?"

You see, it was a family of talking coyotes.

I said, "You and your friends are making a lot of noise."

"We do that," he said. "We're coyotes. We're a very expressive and exuberant type of animal."

I said, "All this ruckus is disturbing the neighborhood."

He said, "I remember one day not too long ago when we were trying to sleep and you had a bunch of people in your back yard who were very vociferous, too."

They were a family of talking coyotes with sophisticated vocabularies.

I said, "That was the Fourth of July."

"So what?"

"So, it's a celebration. We eat outside and we have fun."

He said, "Big deal. Coyotes eat outside all the time, and we have fun when we're doing it. That's why we make so much noise."

I said, "Well, you're ruining a very lovely neighborhood."

He said, "Whoa. Hold it right there. This *was* a lovely neighborhood before you moved in."

I said, "You're kidding. This was nothing but vacant fields."

"To a coyote," he said, "That's a lovely neighborhood."

I said, "I'm sorry, but we're here now and we need our sleep. Cut the noise."

He said, "We were here first."

I said, "Big deal."

He said, "You ruined our lovely neighborhood. In fact, you know where your house stands?"

I said, "Of course."

He said, "That's where the wife and I spent our honeymoon."

I said, "Well, you know, times change. That's progress."

He said, "What do coyotes need with progress? We need food. We need a place to roam, to raise our pups."

"We do, too," I said. "That's why we expand, build more houses."

He said, "Well, we're not expanding. That's why we're going to yip, yap, yelp, bark, howl and do whatever we like for as long as we can."

I said, "Oh, you will, huh? We'll just see about that. We paid a lot of money for that house and you're ruining it for us."

He said, "For us this land was free and you're ruining it for us by building your expensive houses."

I said, "And you and yours should stay away from those houses. You don't belong down there. You come very close to our back fence and you scare the family dog."

He didn't care for that admonition.

He said, "First of all, we got along very well for a long time without any fences to go near. Second of all, when you come out of the house in the morning in that ratty bathrobe of yours and those funny looking fur-lined slippers, you scare our coyote pups."

When I got back in my bedroom my wife asked, "Did you talk to them?"

"Yes I did."

"Are they going to stop making noise?"

"No," I said.

"Boy," she said. "Some people are just so inconsiderate."

"It's funny," I said. "That's the last thing the coyote said to me before I left."

2) The idea should be recognizable:

The basic premise of your humorous article should be so recognizable that readers can say, "Yes! That has happened to me." Certainly in the previous example, everyone has had an experience where they were frustrated playing the "push the button" game while phoning some company. The reader is familiar with that idea, knows about it, has done it.

The "coyote" article is probably not something readers have done, but they know enough about it to identify with it. Readers should at least be able to say, "I understand your point, and I agree with it."

Humor is intensified when it touches the listeners, when they can recognize themselves in the same situation, when they know they've done the same thing you're talking about.

As an example, here's a piece that I wrote for *Arizona Highways*. It generated quite a bit of reader response.

Saguaro Images

It's interesting driving into the Sonoran Desert in the southwestern part of Arizona. The saguaro seem to entice you in. First you spot an isolated saguaro or two. Then you spot clumps of them. Soon they dominate the landscape.

On a recent motor trip along Interstate 10, my wife commented on them. "Aren't the saguaro cactuses beautiful?"

"Yes," I said.

She asked, "Do you use 'cactuses' or 'cacti'?"

I told her, "I don't use either."

She said, "Well, if you see three beautiful saguaros in the desert and you want to write about it, how do you say it."

I say, "I saw a beautiful cactus today. And right next to it were two more just like it."

She said, "Well, I say 'cactuses,' and I love them. I find them very entertaining as I drive along. It's almost as if they were actors out there in the sand putting on a little play for us."

I said, "Do you want me to drive for a while?"

She said, "No, I mean it. For instance, look at that one over there. Do you see it?"

There were hundreds of cactuses in the area she had indicated. Or to be grammatically correct, there was one cactus over there and ninety-nine others just like it in the vicinity. I said, "Which one?"

She said, "The one with its two arms raised heavenward."

They all seemed to have two arms raised heavenward, but I said, "Yeah, I see it."

She said, "It looks like just like a Jesuit reciting his morning prayers."

I said, "Are you sure you don't want me to drive for awhile?" I had seen in some John Wayne movies how the desert sun can drive you insane.

She said, "Doesn't it look like a Jesuit praying?"

I said, "No."

She said, "It does."

I said, "First of all, priests wear long black robes, not green robes with sharp needles sticking out all over them. Second, it's now three-thirty in the afternoon, why is he saying his morning prayers? Third, why is it a Jesuit?"

My wife said, "Just because it makes the image more vivid.

Use your imagination. C'mon, you pick out a cactus and tell me what you see."

I said, "O.K. See that big clump over there on the right."

She said, "Yeah."

I said, "That's a group of Benedictine monks."

She said, "Now you've got it. And what are they doing?"

I said, "They're all saying, 'Let's go get that Jesuit for invading our turf.'"

She said, "Honestly, now. You're just being a wise guy. C'mon, play along with me."

She pointed out another interesting saguaro. "Over there," she said. "There's one with his two arms out and pointing downward."

"Yeah? What's that?" I asked, trying to sound as if I cared.

She said, "That's an umpire in a baseball game. It's a close game, the runner is trying to score and that saguaro is the home plate umpire who's calling him 'out.'"

I said, "That's interesting."

She said, "Then you can visualize it?"

I said, "Sure. But I'll tell you who I really feel sorry for."

She asked, "Who?"

I said, "The poor baseball player who had to slide into home in a field full of cactus. That poor boy will be pulling thorns out of his bottom from now until the World Series is over."

My wife said, "You have absolutely no soul, do you know that? There is a beautiful pageant being played out there in the desert and you're refusing to see it."

I said, "I see gorgeous plants and flowers, but I don't see praying priests who might be knocked over by baseball players sliding through their monastery."

She wouldn't surrender. "Look at that tall, straight saguaro over there."

Again, most of them were tall and straight.

She said, "His arm is bent up and back toward his head."

I said, "Yeah." No enthusiasm.

She said, "He's a soldier blowing taps for his fallen comrades. It's very touching."

I ruined the moment by pointing out that that "soldier" had no "bugle" in his "hand" and also by noting that in all of history there has never been a war in which saguaro cactuses were drafted into military service.

My wife said, "Do you know there's a theory about the brain where the left side is used for practical thinking—things like doing math and figuring out logic?"

I said I didn't know much about it, but I'd heard the idea.

She said, "And the right side of the brain is for imagination, creativity. It's where daydreams and fantasies flourish."

I said, "Yeah?" knowing more was coming.

She said, "Some people use the right side of their brain and some the left."

"So?" I said.

She said, "I think you use the crack that runs down the middle of them."

We didn't play any more games for the rest of that trip. But I must confess that as I looked out the window, many of the saguaros appeared to be holding their sides and laughing at me.

Why did this piece get so many "Letters to the Editor"? Because readers related to it. In their letters people confessed that they too pictured different images as they gazed at the saguaros. It's essential that your humor touch the readers in some way.

3) Whenever possible, the idea should be localized:

Once when I worked on a pilot script for Paramount, the top studio executive came in to watch a rehearsal of the show and to evaluate it. Afterwards, he and his assistant met with the producers and the writers for notes. The top studio executive did most of the talking because…well…because he was the top studio executive. However, his lackey threw in some key thoughts every so often.

The top studio executive would say, "I want the people in this story to be somewhat rebellious, but at the same time to cooperate as much as possible." The lackey would say, "I've got it. You want them to be rebelliously cooperative." The TSE would say, "Exactly."

We writers would jot that down as a note.

Then the TSE might say, "I want the kids to dress kind of shabbily, you know, but also, they should look rather distinguished." The lackey would add, "I think what we want is for them to be fashionably unfashionable."

We writers made another note.

The meeting continued like this through pages and pages of notes. When we finally began our rewriting session, we realized that we had pages and pages of oxymorons. We had demands that were impossible to meet. It

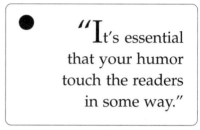

"It's essential that your humor touch the readers in some way."

was as if the top studio executive had said, "I want this figure to be completely round, yet still have some corners." The lackey would shout, "I think we're looking here for a square circle."

We writers would write that down and later realize it was impossible.

I tell this tale here because even today it strikes me as funny, but also because I know that's how some of you must feel about this heading. In the preceding discussion, I recommended that your idea should have universal recognizability. Now I'm suggesting that your premise touch only a limited audience. Like the TSE and his lackey, it feels like I'm asking you to come up with a square circle.

Not really. It is possible to conceive of a premise that has universal appeal to your particular audience or your readership. If you can do that, you'll have a strong basis for your humor. People like to have material written just for them or about their profession or circumstances.

For instance, suppose the golfers at your country club are having an awards banquet and they hire a humorous speaker. The members will laugh more readily at golf jokes than generic gags. They'll laugh harder if the gags are about their head pro or are specific to their own golf course. They'd probably be disappointed if the humorist spoke only on general topics—traffic, cell phones, or whatever.

The speaker in this case would benefit from having content that has universal appeal to this particular audience.

Bob Hope capitalized on this when he visited military bases. He wanted jokes about *this* base. He wanted his writers to supply comic lines about this specific commanding officer, about *these* people in *this* audience—*their* duties, *their* recreation, *their* problems. That was my job for many years on these military jaunts. I would circulate among the servicemen and women and find out what they were talking about, what their complaints were, what their hopes were. Then I'd have to write jokes about those topics for that evening's show.

Certainly Hope did universally recognized monologues, too. He talked about the headlines, the politicians, the celebrities, current fads. He joked about whatever people were talking about. But he knew that the more he could focus his material on a particular audience, the bigger the laughs would be.

To create solid humorous premises, you should try to focus your ideas on as small an audience as you can—again, I add, whenever that's possible.

Below is an example. It's an article from a speaker's magazine. It has universal appeal to a limited audience—to speakers and aspiring speakers.

Give the Speaker a Hand

A survey taken by somebody somewhere once listed "Speaking in Public" as the number one fear of people. Folks fear speaking in public more than anything. More than being attacked by a giant squid. More than getting your lip caught under a manhole cover. More than anything.

I've overcome that fear because I do a lot of banquet speaking. It's a way of curing the ham in me. Sometimes I like to actually hear the laughter and the applause. Other times, I get my exercise running from irritated audiences. Either way, I enjoy public speaking.

But I remember my first attempt.

I learned two things the first time I spoke in public. I learned that I had hands and that I had no idea what the heck I should do with them.

I looked at my hands hanging down at my side and I said to myself, "Why did I bother to bring these?"

They felt like an appendix or tonsils. They probably serve some useful purpose on the human body, but at that particular moment, I couldn't figure out what that might be.

I hadn't even begun to speak, yet I panicked. I knew that everyone in the auditorium was staring at my hands—including me. In fact, I think, people who weren't even supposed to be at my talk poked their heads in the door just to take a look at my hands. I had never really noticed these particular appendages before. I took them for granted. Now, I studied them. I learned, for instance, that my hands were approximately twelve times the size of my head. That's right, they were huge. And they weighed eighty-four pounds each.

I forgot about my notes and my audience and concentrated only on those hands. They grew larger, and heavier, and they seemed to get further and further from my shoulders. That's right. They were actually growing closer to the floor.

They were an embarrassment and I had no idea what to do with them. They no longer fit into my pockets. Then I thought: Hey, why not use them for gesturing? Great idea.

So I decided to begin my speech (I hadn't started talking yet) with a sweeping motion of my hand. It wouldn't move. It just hung there. I thought maybe I'd make the sweeping motion with my other hand (a good speaker should always be ambidextrous), but the other one wouldn't move, either.

These were my hands. They were hanging from my shoulders, but someone must be operating them with a remote control device. I certainly had no influence over them.

I did notice that when I turned my shoulders slightly, they swayed. If I turned my shoulders more, they swayed harder and further. So I did that for a while. The audience checked their programs. Was this a speaker or a puppet show?

I had to say something, so I began. I said, "Uhhhhmmmm," and I kept saying that for about a minute. Until finally someone towards the back yelled, "We can't hear you." The microphone was too low to pick up my voice.

I panicked even more. How could I adjust the microphone? I couldn't use my hands. I couldn't lift them that far. They now weighed 104 pounds each. That's right, they had gained twenty pounds in that short time. So I bent at the knees and at the waist and spoke directly into the microphone.

Beginning again, I repeated, "Uhhhhmmmm" for those who hadn't heard it the first time. In my Groucho Marx-like stance, with my knuckles scraping the floor, I continued my speech.

It failed miserably. The opening "Uhhhhmmmm" was the highlight of my presentation.

Since this speech was to a group of recovering senior citizens at a convalescent home, I thought I had an appropriate finish, at least. I said to them. "Goodbye, and I hope you all get better soon."

A lady sitting in the front row said, "We hope you do, too."

That's when I learned that people were right to fear speaking more than dying. Sometimes they're very similar.

Some may ask the question, "Shouldn't the premise be funny?" Not necessarily. Getting a runaround from a company's phone process is not funny; neither is having coyotes keeping you awake at night. Giving a terrible speech is not a hilarious premise. The humorist must find the comedy that's contained in any premise. The situation doesn't generate the humor; the humorist does.

Chapter Four

How to Get Ideas for Humorous Articles

Every so often inspiration strikes—an idea just pops into the head of a writer. Sometimes the spark is so powerful that the story or the article almost writes itself. The scribe simply sits at the keyboard and types whatever the muse dictates.

Supposedly, Robert Louis Stevenson was once violently ill and almost comatose with a fever for several days. Who knows what bizarre thoughts burned in his mind through that ordeal? When he awoke, the story says, he wrote *Dr. Jekyll and Mr. Hyde* in one sitting.

If the writing gods motivate you, whether with a random thought, a dream, or a torment like Robert Louis Stevenson's, grab that gift. Get it on paper, sell it to the most generous buyer, and be grateful to whomever or whatever sent that project your way.

When I worked in Hollywood, the writers claimed that good premises floated around in the ether and all we had to do was tune into them. One writer complained, "If that's true, then why are all the ideas floating around Neil Simon's house?"

Inspiration is a part of writing. It's one of the better parts of it, actually. Hardly anything is more rewarding than suddenly, from somewhere, getting an idea that you know will work, that you are confident you can write, and that you're positive will sell. It's kind of like getting a hole-in-one in golf.

The problem with inspiration is that it's neither steady nor dependable. Professional writers must turn out product at a reasonably steady rate because our bills must be paid at an unreasonably steady rate. The writing gods don't work to a deadline; professional writers do. If we have an article due on Monday, we can't wait until Thursday for the spirits to move us.

One writer once explained why television staff writers could not afford the luxury of writer's block. The show must go on the air, and a script must be written. He said, "I can turn in a good script on Friday or I can turn in a bad script on Friday. But I can't turn in *no* script on Friday."

Writers don't exactly earn their bread by the proverbial sweat of their brow because writing doesn't produce much brow perspiration. We do, though, earn our livelihood with the material that we produce. Tiger Woods would be a pauper today if he made his living solely from holes-in-one.

If we writers can't rely on salable concepts being Fed-exed or mentally faxed to us from another dimension, our only recourse is to discover ideas on our own. What's an effective and efficient way to do this?

We can begin by realizing that humorists don't *create* humor; we *uncover* it. We're like gold prospectors. They don't create gold. The gold is already in the ground. It has been there for centuries. The prospector searches for the hidden vein. When he finds it, he digs and claws and scratches out the valuable nuggets. That's what humorists must do—find the humor and then extract it.

> "We can begin by realizing that humorists don't *create* humor; we *uncover* it. We're like gold prospectors."

One difference, though, is that gold is not everywhere; humor is. There's fun in practically everything. If we dig deep enough and work hard enough, we'll find it.

How do we do that? With FOCUS.

Focus means to think more and more about less and less. A specialist in medicine is an example. A doctor knows a good deal about your body and those things that can go wrong with it, but a specialist is presumed to know even more about certain parts of your body. A cardiologist, for example, is better educated about the heart. So, specialists know more and more about less and less. Taking this to its extreme, the most brilliant person in the world would be someone who knows everything there is to know about absolutely nothing.

But that's what focus is. It's uncovering and then isolating different facets of your subject matter. By zeroing in on various components, you can concentrate on them and perhaps discover ironies that may not be apparent from the broader view.

Let me give you a practical example of how this works.

I began my comedy writing career by doing friendly, funny roasts about people I worked with. I would emcee banquets for retirement parties, twenty-five year celebrations, even farewell dinners. In effect, I would be writing a short, humorous article about the guest of honor. At first, I was kidding people that I knew fairly well. I knew them well enough to write some funny material about them. Eventually, though, I would emcee dinners for people I wasn't acquainted with.

Imagine being asked to write a funny piece about Charlie Wilson when you don't know Charlie Wilson. It's not easy. I didn't know anything about Charlie Wilson. I may never have met Charlie Wilson.

I would have to reduce Charlie Wilson to his component parts. I needed to focus on different aspects of Charlie. My first step would be to get a biography on Mr. Wilson. Where is he from? What schools did he go to? What departments in the company has he worked in? What bosses has he worked for? Has he won any awards? What is his present position in the company? Any one or several of these might provide fodder for some humorous kidding about Charlie.

My next step would be to call a meeting with several of Charlie's friends. I'd say, "Tell me something about your pal, Charlie, so that we can have some fun with him at his retirement party. What do you folks kid him about? What does he kid himself about? What are his hobbies? Has anything embarrassing happened to him here at work that we can talk about?" Folks can be surprisingly candid when they know it's for some good-natured fun.

If possible, I would get together with his family and ask them the same sort of questions.

Eventually, I would develop some good ammunition to use "against" Charlie at his retirement celebration. This research would offer me several areas that I could focus on for humorous ideas.

Let's suppose the consensus was that good old Charlie Wilson was a tightwad. Great. Now I can concentrate on that area. I can focus on that facet. I can generate some comedy based on that idea.

Charlie's pretty tight with a buck, you know. On their very first date, he took Marie out for coffee and donuts. Marie was thrilled. She had never donated blood before.

Another area might be that Charlie is an incurable pipe smoker and is constantly fiddling with his pipe. Also, he and Marie have seven children. That's an area for some ribbing, too.

Before the banquet I was talking to Charlie's wife, Marie. I asked her if it bothered her that Charlie was constantly fiddling with his pipe. She said, "Not at all. After seven children I'm happy with anything that keeps his hands busy."

The entire process is thinking more and more about less and less. I sliced Charlie Wilson into segments. It's almost like those posters you would see of a steer with dotted lines showing the different cuts of meat. I butchered Charlie into various "cuts." This served two purposes. First, it would give me ideas to talk about. I now had something to say about good old Charlie Wilson. Second, it allowed me to concentrate on those areas separately. It's much easier to write a funny bit about Charlie Wilson's *stinginess* than it is to write a funny bit about Charlie Wilson. That's the value of focus.

As a result of this process, I could always come up with a thousand-word humorous essay about the guest of honor. I would always go back to the friends and family and have them review the piece to make sure that nothing in there was offensive to the guest of honor or his family, who generally attended the banquet.

In fact once, as the emcee, I told the family, "Please don't be offended by anything we say tonight about your dad. We're only kidding. In fact, many of the nice things we say about him tonight aren't true, either."

Focusing works not only with people but with any premise you must write about. Investigate different areas of your topic. Break it into several components. Then break those components down to find the humor in them. By doing this you'll improve both the quantity and the quality of your output.

Once in an experiment with some writing students, I had them write a humorous piece about a well-known foreign beach resort that none of them had ever visited. Writing about a place you've never been is like writing about a person you don't know.

They each did their research and came up with several creative ideas for humorous pieces. One did an article about taking one of those wind-surfing jaunts towed by a boat over the surf. Another wrote about the various fancy drinks they served at this resort and the fancy prices attached to them. Someone else did a piece about conversing with people in a foreign language. Each one found some aspect of this place to feature and had fun with it.

The humor, like the gold in the ground, is there. We have to find it and extract it.

In the following chapters, we'll explore several ways of FOCUSING.

But before we do that, let's discuss this concept of focusing a bit more and be clear about how it relates to the humor writing process. Let's be sure we know what it can do and what it can't do.

What it can do is help to make the conditions right for the creative process to happen. Here's an example of that. In one of my comedy writing classes, I asked the attendees to write some jokes on a specific topic. At that time, a major item in the news was that Queen Elizabeth II was visiting then President Ronald Reagan at his ranch in Santa Barbara, California. The media made a big deal about their being scheduled to go horseback riding together. However, heavy rains in the area brought flash floods and potential mud slides and put the ride in jeopardy. I asked the people in the class to write jokes about this.

They produced very few gags and the ones they did produce were weak. The subject was too broad.

Now I gave them some focus. Our premise now was much narrower—they were going to ride, but they would have to find horses that were specially equipped in some way to deal with the weather. Write jokes about those animals.

With that focus established, they came up with more gags and stronger gags.

...they did go riding and the ride was easy. The hard part was first teaching the horses how to use the scuba gear.

...they went riding. First they had to scour the entire area to find two horses with gills.

...they did go riding. Fortunately at Reagan's ranch they happened to have two stallions that had webbed hooves.

...there was one scary incident during the ride. One of the horses was spooked by a shark.

Now that last gag didn't stick to the concept we had established, but that's all right. Sometimes thinking creatively in one area can lead to creative thinking in another area. The object is to produce humor, not stick to a rigid set of rules.

So what this focus concept did was set up certain conditions which helped uncover some comedy. However, it didn't *write* any of those jokes. It simply prepared the conditions so that those jokes would evolve.

What this concept can't do—and what no one or nothing can do— is write the humor for you.

At another lecture I gave on writing humor, one persistent questioner kept coming back to this idea. "But how do you write the joke?" she would ask. I'd ramble on again about narrowing the attack and area and focusing on various facets of the topic.

"Okay," she would ask, "But how do you write the joke?"

After she went back to this several more times, I finally said, "Let's forget about humor for a bit and grow some beans." That confounded her so much that she allowed me to make my point.

Writing humor using this concept of focusing is like growing beans. If you want a small vegetable patch in your back yard, you would first prepare the soil. I'm not much of a gardener, but I suppose you would till it and turn it and soften it up for the planting.

Next, of course, you would get some seeds and plant them according to the directions, spaced so far apart and set so deep into the ground. After that, you'd have to care for the ground—fertilize it and water it. You want to provide perfect conditions for that seed to germinate. You can do all you can to make conditions ideal.

But you can't grow the bean.

When that bean germinates and tiny green leaves break the surface, that's a mini-miracle that you have no control over. All you can do is provide the right atmosphere for that mini-miracle to happen.

Humor writing is similar. You control the conditions and allow the humor to happen. When it does, it's just as much a mini-miracle as the bean coming to life.

The point to remember, though, is that you'll get more beans and healthier beans if you do prepare the soil, rather than if you just sprinkle the seeds on unprepared sod.

That basically is the purpose and the function of focus.

Now let's move on to these chapters on ways to focus specifically.

Chapter Five

Focus on Topics

Being a writer on *The Tonight Show*, furnishing monologue material to Johnny Carson was an enviable gig in television writing. It was a steady weekly paycheck all year long. Most television shows only did twenty-two to twenty-six shows a year. When the season ended, you either had to find work during the hiatus or do without a paycheck. Not with *The Tonight Show*. That was year-round.

Carson's show, too, was very dependable. It scored good ratings and made money for the network. There was no worry about the show being canceled. Other shows always faced that possibility, even the successful ones.

It was a prestigious show, also. Viewers liked it. People in the industry respected it. A writer on that show was proud to be a writer on that show. There were other shows writers earned good incomes from, but that they really didn't want to talk about.

But there had to be a downside to writing comedy for Johnny Carson night after night. I spoke with Carson's head writer once and asked him about that. I suggested that it might be hard to come up with good comedy lines night after night. He said that the lines weren't the problem. Good comedy writers can come up with funny material about almost anything. The hard part was coming up with enough current topics to be funny about. Each night Carson might do monologue material on five or six different subjects. It was difficult for the writers to comb the newspapers and magazines to find interesting subjects to kid about.

It's a problem in writing humorous articles, too. Most of us feel that we can be funny about almost anything. The problem can be finding that specific something that we can be funny about.

When we have trouble finding something to be funny about or when we can't be funny about whatever we're trying to be funny about, we call that "writer's block." I knew one writer who ridiculed this malady. He said that only writers were arrogant enough to have a name for not wanting to write. He said there were no such things as "plumber's block," "accountant's block," or "good humor man's block."

He made his point further by having you imagine that you were on a trip somewhere. You had fought with lines of traffic, lugged your baggage through large airports, endured the searches at the metal detectors, waited impatiently for delayed flights. Finally, you arrive in your destination city. You flag down a cab, jump in the back seat, and say to the driver, "Take me to the Sheraton Hotel."

The cab driver turns to you and says, "Sorry, Pally, I can't take you there."

You're stunned. You say, "Why not?"

He says, "I've got cab driver's block."

It sounds ridiculous, doesn't it? Well, this writer's contention was that it was just as ridiculous for us to hide behind the so-called writer's block.

Yet we all know that there are times when we can't think of anything to write about or we can't think of anything clever to say about what we want to write about. When that happens we have to do something about it. If you're facing a deadline, you'd better think of something to write about and get some words on paper or you're going to have an angry editor calling.

I find there are two main reasons for freezing up creatively. One is that we're secretly afraid of the project we're starting. We want to write the Great American Novel or we want to do a funny piece for the Op-Ed page. So we reach our hands out to the keyboard to begin and our subconscious whispers, "I'm not good enough to do this." So our fingers lock up. We don't want to begin the project because we feel that the end result will be embarrassing. Those who read it will know that we weren't good enough to pull this off.

It's like the example that you often hear about walking along a board that's two feet wide and ten feet long. Any normal person could walk across that with no problem. But…suspend that same board between two buildings ten stories high, and the prospect becomes a tad more intimidating. We now have something to fear in failing. The same happens when we writers have a fear of failing.

If this happens, you have to schedule a pep-talk with yourself. Review your past writing. Remind yourself that you've written funny pieces before and many of them about topics tougher to handle than this one. Convince yourself that you can do it and then do it.

Another inspirational angle is to read some writers that you admire and respect. See how well they handled their assignment. You know that it can be done. So again, you sit down and do it.

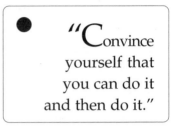

"Convince yourself that you can do it and then do it."

Many of my colleagues on Bob Hope's writing staff would often get themselves in the mood for writing by slipping in a tape of Bob Hope delivering a comedy monologue. They'd listen to the gags and Hope's masterful delivery and timing and eventually, they'd get into the rhythm of the comedy and sit down and start cranking out one-liners.

Another thing that can trigger writer's block (which my writer friend still insists doesn't exist) is mental fatigue. Sometimes your mind is just weary from working on the same sort of material. It literally shuts down. It's like a boxer who punches himself out in the ring. He has thrown so many punches that he has no power left in his tired arms. He may still flail, but he's not punching effectively.

If this happens to you, take a mini-vacation. Get away from the writing process for a while. Watch a movie, take a walk, take a nap, call a friend…do anything except write or think about writing. I have found that even if I have a pressing deadline, I can sometimes get my work done faster by not getting the work done immediately.

Often, you'll discover that while you're concentrating on other things—golf, a crossword puzzle, or whatever—your subconscious will continue to concentrate on your writing assignment. Frequently, I'll take a break from an assignment that has worn me out and come back to the task with fresh ideas that just pop into my head.

One other antidote for so-called writer's block is simply to write. Some authors recommend retyping the last page that they worked on earlier. It gets them used to putting words on paper again. Or you can force yourself to write out notes. Again, it gets you either writing or typing and it gets your mind going again. Or simply start writing. Even if it's terrible, you can always crumple that sheet up, throw it in the waste basket, and start your *real* writing with a fresh sheet of paper.

One former associate of mine had a unique way of getting his "heart started." He would begin each morning by composing a limerick. He felt that when his mind was conditioned to write an acceptable short poem, it was ready to begin the day's task of turning out humor.

Now that we agree that writer's block is not an incurable disease, let's begin the process of focusing on potential areas of humor that we can write about. This first procedure features different areas on which to focus to find humorous premises.

Your own memory

This is the obvious place to look for material, but as we discussed earlier, the obvious is often overlooked. Sometimes, though, by focusing on this particular area, you can extract the humor that's been lying dormant for years.

I've always been fascinated by some of the reunions I've enjoyed with fellow writers. We gather for lunch or cocktails and invariably someone will begin to tell a funny story about some experience we had together. Then another will jump in with an anecdote following up on that first one. Another writer will jump in with a sequel to that tale. The stories go on and on. Many of us tell tales that we hadn't told in years and in fact had almost forgotten.

You have many stories in your memory, too. One writer, during a vacation, took along a notepad and as he lay on the beach each day, he would concentrate only on funny tales from his past. He came back with a wealth of material for humorous articles.

Personal relationships

Kids are always saying funny things. Husbands and wives have incidents that they laugh about. Sometimes they fume about them at the time, but discover they are laughable later. My wife enjoys doing the crossword puzzles in the newspapers each Sunday morning. I hate crossword puzzles. If the puzzle asks for a five-letter word and all I can think of is an eight-letter word, I just write smaller. But my wife will always volunteer my help. She'll ask, "Who was a hall-of-fame basketball player from Villanova University?"

"I don't know," I say. I don't want to get involved.

"It begins with an 'A'," she says. I am involved.

Now I remember that there was a famous ballplayer from Villanova. He played for the Philadelphia Warriors years ago and was a standout. The only problem is I can't remember his name.

"How many letters?" I ask.

"Six," she says.

"Do you have any other letters?" I ask.

"No," she says.

I'm thinking...Arbuckle? Archer? Albrecht? They're all wrong, but I'm obsessed now with remembering this famous athlete.

My day is ruined, but my wife just casts it aside and continues merrily on with the crossword from another paper or watching her cooking shows.

This can make for a funny humorous piece.

Also, my wife and I are constantly arguing about whether she told me something and I've forgotten it or whether she forgot to tell me something and now I'm taking the blame for having forgotten something she never told me.

Try to recall stories with you and your parents. Recall some tales about your siblings. My brother is constantly calling after some of my articles appear in magazines and threatening to sue me for libel or have me committed to an institution for the criminally comedic. How about your in-laws? You and your boss? You and your fellow workers? Your friends? Your enemies?

There's plenty of ammunition for fun there. Find it.

Newspaper and magazines

Most of the material we wrote when I was on Bob Hope's writing staff was from the daily headlines. If some big news broke, we'd get a phone call shortly thereafter. One of Hope's staff writers was married to a Los Angeles policeman. One morning a disastrous earthquake hit the area, and the LAPD immediately began calling all of its officers to report to duty. This writer received a call from Bob Hope to do some earthquake lines *before* the emergency call from the police department.

Some mornings, I'd glance at the headlines and know they were pregnant with comedy topics. I often felt like rushing over to Bob Hope's house, grabbing the newspaper off his doorstep, and burying it before he had a chance to read it. It might get me out of some work.

However, it's not just the headlines that furnish fodder for humorous articles. Some of the tidbits hidden in small paragraphs on the inside pages can trigger your imagination, too.

Read through magazines and newspapers, but be aware as you read them. Make some notes. They could provide the raw material for several of your funny pieces. At one of our writing conferences, a faculty member suggested an exercise that the attendees could work on during the year. He recommended that they select certain topics from the daily paper's front pages and do some comedy work on those. After that, they should randomly select topics from the front pages. Then they should graduate to opening the newspaper to any page and randomly select topics there. It was good training on writing comedy on any assignment.

What people are talking about

On news programs now we're inundated with the latest polls. Here's how many people who think the president is doing a good job. Here's how many people who think he's not doing a good job. Here's how many people who think the economy is our number one priority. Here's how many think defense should be our primary concern. Politicians and news people are always interested in knowing what people are thinking.

As humorists, we should be aware of that, too. The funniest articles are often the ones that concern themselves with what people are thinking.

One time I had to turn in a humorous article by end of day. It was a Saturday and I wanted to play my three or four hours of tennis in the morning. I also wanted to watch John McEnroe who was playing at Wimbledon and the match would be televised. McEnroe was quite controversial during this particular Wimbledon tourney. He was arguing and throwing tantrums and getting big ratings for the telecast. Even my wife and youngsters, who didn't normally watch tennis on TV, wanted to watch that afternoon's matches.

I had to come up with something to write about, but couldn't. I played my morning tennis and all the guys were discussing McEnroe's behavior. I rushed home after my workout so that I could get ready to watch the Wimbledon matches, even though I still didn't have anything to write about.

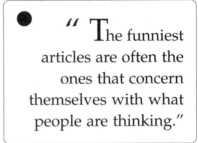

" The funniest articles are often the ones that concern themselves with what people are thinking."

My kids were in front of the TV and eager for me to join them to watch the tennis. I felt guilty, but I was going to watch the tournament even though I still hadn't come up with a topic for my deadline.

When I complained that I should be in my office getting a premise instead of watching John McEnroe misbehaving in London, one of my daughters said, "Why don't you write about John McEnroe's behavior at Wimbledon?"

Everyone was talking about it, but I had completely overlooked it.

Listen to what people are saying and use it.

Pet peeves

This is not only a good area to explore for humor, but it's also cathartic. Is someone or something bothering you? Get your revenge by writing a scathing humorous article about it. It's good for your writing soul.

Do cell phones in restaurants annoy you? Good. Tell the world about it. Did the woman in the seat next to you chatter about herself all the way to Dallas? Make that imbecile the star of your next humorous piece.

It's good to be angry when you're writing humor. It gives a little extra zip to your verse.

So if you're searching for something to write about, make a list of the things that get your goat. Remember that if these things bother you, they probably irritate a goodly percentage of your readers, too. And the editors!

Personal observation

Take a good long look at yourself in the mirror. There's comedy staring back at you from that looking glass. Gaze inside your mind. There are some bizarre things going on in there. Look at yourself in general and you'll get material for many humorous pieces.

Be honest. Are you putting on a little bit of weight around the middle? Are you having a hard time staying on a diet? That may be bad for your physical fitness, but it might do wonders for your comedy repertoire.

I was once intrigued by the fact that I wanted to do certain things on the tennis court that I used to be able to do but now my body didn't seem to agree with me. I did a piece in which I was playing tennis. My opponent would hit a shot and I would mentally say, "Turn to your left, take two quick steps, and rifle that ball back cross court for a winner." My mind would say, "Hold it. Let's think a little longer and harder about those two quick steps." The ball would sail past me. It was a funny piece about me realizing that I was getting a tad too old to be an athlete.

Observe what's going on with you…in your life. It's probably happening to many of the people who read your stuff. Dig into it and you'll find lots of areas for humor.

Chapter Six

Focus on Time

Let's get a bit more surgical about searching for material.

I always get a kick out of the way courtroom attorneys can whittle away at the person testifying until they get the answer they want.

The attorney asks, "What time did you hear the dog barking?"

The witness responds, "I'm not sure."

"You did hear the dog barking, didn't you?"

"Yes, I definitely did."

"Well, what time was it when you first heard the barking."

The witness repeats, "I'm not sure. I wasn't really paying attention to the time."

The lawyer asks, "Was it light outside?"

"No, it was dark."

"Then it must have been after 6 P.M. because that's when the sun went down that day."

The witness agrees. "Oh, yes, it was definitely after six o'clock."

The attorney presses on. "How much after six o'clock was it?"

"I don't know."

"Well, was it midnight?"

"Oh no, it wasn't midnight."

Now the attorney is getting somewhere. "Could it have been around nine o'clock?"

The witness concedes, "It might have been."

"Could it have been later than nine?"

The defendant guesses. "I don't think it was."

The lawyer moves in. "So it was between 6 P.M. and 9 P.M."

"Yeah."

"Was it closer to six or closer to nine?"

"I think it was closer to nine."

"Could we say it was between eight and nine?"

"Yeah, I guess we could."

"Closer to eight or to nine?"

"I would guess it was closer to eight."

"Could we say 8:10 P.M.?"

"Probably a little later than that."

"How about 8:20 P.M.?"

"Yeah, it might have been around 8:20 P.M."

The attorney says, "So at 8:20 P.M. you heard the dog bark?"

The witness says, "Yeah, that's right."

From that moment on, let the record show that this witness who didn't know what time it was when he heard the dog bark now is locked in to hearing the dog bark at precisely twenty minutes after eight in the evening.

Pretty clever, huh?

Sometimes we humorists can find potential material by dividing time surgically like this apocryphal interrogator did. Remember the principle of focusing is that we divide potential subject matter into smaller and smaller parts.

One obvious division is by months. January prompts ideas related to the New Year. February not only has Valentine's Day, but also many significant birthdays—Washington's, Lincoln's, Thomas Edison's, and others. March is famous for its windy season. April 1 inspires not only professional humorists, but amateur pranksters, too. May contains Mother's Day. June is a favorite of brides. July is Independence Day and picnics. August is when the leaves start turning colors. September is the traditional back-to-school month. October, of course, is when kids dress up and go trick or treating for Halloween. November is the month in which we give thanks. December is the month when Santa tours the world handing out gifts.

Each of these topics, if you focus on it, can be subdivided into smaller facets. For example, Valentine's Day in February can inspire humor related to buying gifts for your sweetie, getting gifts from your loved one, handing out Valentine cards when you were in school, getting or not getting many Valentine cards from your school chums, Cupid, and countless other areas related to the February 14 holiday.

You can also divide the year into its four seasons. Summer might bring to mind thoughts of vacations, going to the beach, and getting out of school. Winter reminds you of snow, snowball fights, skiing, cold evenings and warm fires. Spring, of course, is a time of renewal, fresh flowers, pretty dresses, baseball. Fall is when the leaves start turning, they fall and need to be raked, the days grow longer and colder.

These ideas only scratch the surface. You should recognize that by dividing time into its various facets you can concentrate your thinking and generate potential areas that you can write about.

You can get even more clinical with time, though, and generate material from your own daily experiences. A comedian I once worked for used to introduce a story by saying, "You know, you always hear comedians saying, 'A funny thing happened to me on the way to the theater.' I've been coming to the theater for twenty-eight years now and nothing funny ever happened to me...until tonight."

That may be how you feel about your ordinary days—nothing funny ever happens to you. But if you take a closer look at it, maybe it does. If you really focus on your day, you might be able to find some creative material in there.

Again, humor is often finding the obvious that is consistently overlooked. If you thoroughly investigate your daily life, you might surprise yourself with the comedy you can generate from it. And you might be surprised to find that humor is contained in the daily lives of many other people, too.

How do we start searching out this humor?

We begin, once again, by concentrating on smaller sections of your day. Begin by breaking it into three-hour segments. Divide the day into these sections: midnight to 3 A.M., 3 A.M. to 6 A.M., 6 A.M to 9 A.M., 9 A.M. to noon, noon to 3 P.M., 3 P.M. to 6 P.M., 6 P.M. to 9 P.M., and finally 9 P.M. to midnight.

Now when you want to find some topics for your humorous article, you can isolate any one of these areas and focus on it. Analyze it completely. Pull it apart. Think about many of the things that you do during that period and what happens to you as you're doing them. Certainly some concepts will be obvious, but with more focus, you may uncover some items that are there and are fairly obvious, but you hadn't really thought about before. We're searching for those things that are in plain view, but no one seems to see.

Just as an experiment, let's take the period from midnight to 3 A.M. The inclination here is to say that nothing funny, or even potentially funny, happens during that time period. You might say, "I sleep during that time and that's all I do." That's the obvious activity during that time, but humorists get creative by discovering other "obvious" premises.

Let's analyze it just a bit further—focus on it, if you will—and see if we can't uncover some interesting aspects of midnight to three. Yes, you sleep, but how do you sleep? Do you sleep on your back or on your belly? If you sleep on your back, are you superior to those who sleep on their bellies? Maybe there's a funny article in that. Do you sleep soundly? Do some weird noises wake you during this period? Might those noises be a burglar? I once did a humorous piece about just that—my wife heard a suspicious noise and thought it might be an intruder. She said to me, "Go see." The fun in the piece came from my trying to act manly while trying to avoid going down and confronting a dangerous thug. I included one of my articles in chapter 3 called "Neighborly Disagreement." If you take a look back at that piece you'll see that it was about some noises that awoke my wife and me at two o'clock in the morning.

> "Again, humor is often finding the obvious that is consistently overlooked."

Also, you probably dream during this period. Some of those dreams might be part of a funny article. Sometimes I'll have a dream that is so upsetting that it wakes me up. I know it's only a dream and that it never happened, but often, once I'm awake, I try to correct whatever bothered me in the dream. That's funny—a rational wide awake person trying to remedy something that never happened. Maybe that's an article.

Do you talk in your sleep? Have you ever gotten in trouble for something you said in your sleep between midnight and three in the morning? Have you overheard your spouse's ramblings during the night? Might that have led to some problems during breakfast?

You get the idea. We've taken one portion of the day and dissected it. It's a quiet time of the day when nothing seems to be happening, yet with a bit of concentrated effort, we've created some areas that might generate some funny material.

This was only a "top of the head" investigation. If you concentrated more on it and did a thorough brainstorming evaluation, you'd most likely come up with much more material that could be useful in your humor writing.

This is just one portion of your day. You still have seven other three-hour segments that you can mine for material.

Certainly, this is not the only place to get ideas. We're going to talk about several more in upcoming chapters. However, it is one of many methods that you can use when you're stuck for ideas. When you have that writer's block (which some of us argue doesn't exist) this is a way of getting rid of it.

Let's discuss one other thought about time, while we're on the subject, which might be beneficial to writers. Each of us probably has different levels of energy during the day. One of us might work better and more efficiently during the morning, while another prefers the afternoon or evening. As professionals, we often must work when the deadline demands it. However, we're often free to work to our own schedule.

I usually prefer getting my work done early in the day. I seem to perform better then. I even noticed that I played better tennis in the morning than I did in the late afternoon. Why? I have no idea.

I worked with more enthusiasm and produced better material when I attacked the project early in the day. However, for some time I worked on a staff where this was almost impossible. We began our work day at ten in the morning. It was a television show, and show business people don't adhere to banker hours. Businesses would start at eight o'clock; we preferred ten.

We showed up at ten, but we didn't start work at that time. We had our coffee and donuts at the desk, and the group would discuss the TV shows that aired last night, or we'd discuss the ball game, or we'd discuss the latest show business scandal, or we'd discuss whatever anyone felt like discussing. That ate into my ideal productive time.

Then I worked with a partner who was an early riser. He'd wake up at four in the morning, read the paper, go for a jog, take a shower, and show up at work six hours later. By eleven-thirty, he was ready for lunch.

My morning schedule was destroyed. As a professional I had to adjust to the protocol of the workplace. If I had a choice, I would have gotten more work done before lunch.

If you have a choice, you should maximize your work time. Discover when your best working period is. If it's morning, do your writing then, and reserve your record keeping, letter writing, and phone calls for the afternoon hours. If you work better later in the day, get your clerical work done early and save those peak hours for your writing.

One extreme example was a writer who would go to Las Vegas to complete a project. He liked to work almost non-stop when a deadline approached. Vegas, he felt, was perfect for that. He could find a restaurant at any time during the day. He could work until he wearied, then go out for breakfast regardless of the hour. It was a twenty-four hour town, and he wanted to work as many of those twenty-four as he could.

Not a practical example of efficient time use, but an interesting one.

Chapter Seven

Focus on Location

A few years ago, my wife and I toured Italy. We had a wonderful time in a fascinating country. However, I did have a few complaints. For instance, Italy, for some reason, insists on communicating mostly in Italian. It was a strain on me and, to be honest, it was a strain on those people who had to do business with me.

One afternoon, we stopped for cocktails in the hotel bar. I wanted to settle the bill and leave, but when I politely asked the bartender how much I owed, he would say, "Later." I figured he was busy, so I had another cocktail until he could figure out my tab. When I asked him what the bill was again, he said, "Later."

When I was referring to the bar tab and asking "How much?" I was really asking him "When?" The word for "how much" in Italian is "quanto"; the word for "when" is "quando." In Italian the words are very similar. That's very confusing. In English, "when" sounds nothing like "how much." Why don't they just use those instead?

My wife is much smarter than I am about traveling. She knew we'd be traveling through Italy and that Italian is in very common usage over there (I told you she was much smarter about certain things than I am), so she studied the language—enough so that she could converse with the natives.

She taught me a few basic phrases like "Dove e il gabinetto?" That means, "Where is the bathroom?" Very basic. So one day we were finishing up dinner in a pleasant restaurant and I said to my wife, in English, "Where is the bathroom?" She said, in English, "Find out for yourself." She was goading me into using my newly acquired language skills.

So, I left the table and asked one of the waiters, "Dove e il gabinetto?" And he told me...in Italian. He told me in about three minutes worth of Italian, spoken very quickly, of which I understood not a word.

I politely said, "Grazie," and returned to my table and said to my wife, "Dove e il gabinetto?" Then I added, "And tell me in Inglesi, s'il vous plait." That's "tell me" in English, "in English" in Italian, and "please" in either Spanish or French, I'm not sure which.

My wife simply pointed to a sign that said, "Toletta."

Then, of course, I had to come back to our table and ask my wife, "Am I an 'uomo' or a 'donna'?"

All of this became part of an article I did about my vacation.

This is another device you can use to gather ideas for your humorous articles—focus on locations. Break the world into smaller components. The obvious divisions, of course, are the ones that have already been made for you. Continents, countries, states, cities, are all areas that you can explore for humor. Even these divisions can be further dissected. In cities, for example, you can explore restaurants, hotels, and various tourist attractions.

In this previous example, my wife and I vacationed for several weeks in Italy. During that trip, and without detracting from the relaxation, I simply made notes of different sites we saw and various events that we experienced. When I got home, I had plenty of ammunition for several humorous pieces.

Since I do a monthly column for *Arizona Highways*, whenever I travel around the state, I gather interesting information and convert that to short, funny pieces for my column, "Wit Stop."

Often the notes I take are simply used as a starting point for the humor. For example, I visited the Titan Missile Museum in Green Valley, Arizona. That's a fascinating, well-preserved Titan missile base. These bases were a deterrent to hostile missile launches during the Cold War. They're all destroyed now except for this disarmed one in Green Valley. The piece I wrote based on this visit wasn't about missiles, though. It was about a school yard challenge I had to fight the neighborhood bully. The Titan missiles were our nation's defense system. My defense system, in my article, was to try any way I could to get out of confronting this oaf who would probably beat and dismember me with no problem at all.

On another occasion, my family and I visited Meteor Crater which is about thirty-five miles outside of Flagstaff, Arizona. This site is tremendously impressive. It's a hole in the ground about 600 feet deep and 4,100 feet across. It was formed when a meteor about 100 feet in diameter and weighing 50,000 tons smashed into the earth traveling at approximately 43,000 miles per hour. This happened over 49,000 years ago. The article I wrote was not about that meteor, though. It was about my fear of being hit with another meteor while we were vacationing there.

So the ideas were not really tied to the sites I visited, but they were prompted by those places.

In order to get material by focusing on locations, you might begin by reviewing places that you've visited. Think back on your travels to foreign countries, different cities or states, various vacation resorts you've enjoyed. Focus on them and try to extract any humor you can.

As another example, here's a piece I did about visiting a dude ranch in Arizona.

Hopalong Dude

Dateline: Dude Ranch, USA

Clothes, they say, make the man. Cowboy clothes, though, do not make a cowboy.

It was my first morning at the Dude Ranch and I stood, demoralized, before the cruelly honest full-length mirror in my room. My cowboy togs didn't look like rugged western wear, but like a Halloween costume gone bad.

On my shopping spree before this City Slicker vacation, I selected each item carefully hoping that the ensemble would make me look like Gene Autry, Roy Rogers, John Wayne, Clint Eastwood. It didn't. Instead I looked like the stunt double for Moe in "The Three Stooges Go West."

I tried to visualize myself dressed like this in frontier days. I saw myself riding a wagon train across open prairie. Suddenly a few Indians on horseback appeared on the crest of a distant hill. Then several hundred more mounted warriors came into view behind them. In my fantasy, they swooped down at full gallop towards us. Hastily, we drove the wagons into a defensive circle. Women and children loaded rifles and prepared bandages as we men braced for an heroic stand.

Then the Indian chief approached our wagon train and said, "No, no, we're not attacking. We just wanted to get a look at that city guy who's dressed up in the silly cowboy outfit."

The wagon master called me forward and put me on display. The Indians had a good laugh and rode back over the hill, slapping their naked thighs in glee. A few of them laughed so hysterically, they fell off their horses and had to remount. Even their pinto ponies, instead of neighing, bared their huge teeth and sort of chuckled to themselves.

When they got back to their village, they'd send a few smoke signals and the entire episode would be repeated when we reached the next tribe. My pathetic image taunted me from the mirror, I had to admit the Indians were right. I was laughable. If I had lived in the Old West, I would have had to join a nudist camp to avoid looking ridiculous. It's no small confession to admit that one looked less silly naked than in this faux-western garb.

Some can wear cowboy duds; others can't. I was obviously one of the others.

It all started with the hat. I had difficulty finding one to fit. Oh, I don't mean 6 and 7/8 or 7 and 1/8. I could find the right size-size. But I couldn't find a cowboy hat whose shape fit the proportions of my body. If the brim was too big I looked like an alien space craft had just landed on my head. If the crown was too small I looked like I had a felt growth on my noggin that should be lanced. In any case, I wore a ten-gallon hat, eight and a half gallons of which looked just plain dumb.

Then there was the belt buckle. There are basically two kinds of cowboy bellies. There's the flat, washboard like stomach with not an ounce of fat, and there's the huge beer belly where the belt comes around and then under the midsection so the belt buckle looks like Atlas holding up the world. Big metal belt buckles look appropriate on either of those tummy types. Me? I looked like I was holding my pants up with a manhole cover.

And the boots made me look awkward. The heels were so high that I pitched forward. When I moved, I felt like I was walking down an eternal gangplank. When I stood still I looked like the Leaning Tower of Pisa in blue jeans.

The jeans were another problem. Real cowhands wear dusty, faded, well-worn trousers. My jeans were neat, starched, and as blue as a Marine's dress uniform. And they chafed the inside of my thighs something awful. I was the only cowpoke at the ranch who wanted to wear his chaps on the inside.

Between the boots and the denim drawers I walked like a cowboy who was headed downhill to the nearest pharmacist to get something that would cure diaper rash.

But I was paying for this vacation so I endured the sniggering throughout the day. I wore my cow punching togs to the flapjack breakfast, the trail ride, and lunch at the chuck wagon. I kept them on for the afternoon roping lessons, the amateur rodeo, the evening cocktail party and barbecue. I yodeled lustily through the after-dinner sing along, even hollering "Yippee-ki-yo" and waving my hat when instructed to. The hat even looked nerdy when I held it in my hand. When we finally ended with "Happy Trails to You," I felt my day's humiliation was almost over.

But it wasn't.

The wrangler said, "All you cowboys and cowgirls head to the barn right now for this evening's entertainment—line dancing lessons."

More hilarity at my expense.

Finally at day's end, I slipped out of my cowboy clothes and into my pajamas with the little guns and holsters printed all over them. Worn out from the day's ridin', ropin', and ridicule endurin', I slept peacefully and well. I dreamed of myself back home, comfortably dressed in polyester, button-down shirt, and shoes with laces.

Ride 'em, City Slicker.

This shows, too, how limitless the ideas can be. Arizona is a small part of our world. It's about 335 miles wide and 390 miles long. In my writing for *Arizona Highways*, I've produced more than two hundred humorous articles and almost all of them were about some aspect of the state.

Your personal geography

You also have a personal geography that can be explored for humorous ideas. Each day you travel to various locations. You drive the highways, visit shops and markets, go to your workplace, maybe walk or jog around the neighborhood, perhaps you frequent a gym, and you might go to arenas for sporting events. You go to many different places. Focus on these. Make a list of them. Then when you need inspiration for your next funny article, focus on any one of them and extract the humor from it.

I recently read a funny item about a person dreaming about traveling her route to work. This humorist said (and I'm paraphrasing because I'll never find the exact quote) that she dreamed she was on the freeways. She kept swerving and purposely bumping into others driving along her route. She'd smash into one car, then another. She said she wasn't trying to cause any injury; she was just trying to knock the cell phones out of their hands.

There's an idea that's pretty much based on this humorist's personal geography that could be made into an amusing 700 to 800 words.

You might find a lot of fun in the idiosyncrasies of the supermarket where you shop. What are the clerks like? What insane things do the other shoppers do? Can you always find what you're looking for?

I once did an article about visiting a government office—the DMV, Department of Motor Vehicles. I stood in line for an hour (maybe I exaggerated in my article, but that's the writer's privilege) only to find out when I got to the counter that I was in the wrong line. I was sent to another line, waited again, only to find out that the clerk at the first line kept some of the documents that I needed at the second line. I went back and stood in the first line again, only to be told that I couldn't retrieve the missing documents from the first line unless I had a form from the lady at the second line. Well, you get the idea. This farce could continue in my article until I finally heard the clerk say, "Here you go, sir. Here's the registration for your new boat." I was there to register a new car. Back to line one.

There's plenty of material out there, if you break it down into workable segments and then focus on extracting the humor.

There's even a smaller geographical location that you can investigate to uncover funny ideas—your own home. You spend a good portion of your life there, so it owes you some inspiration. Again, though, you must zero in on parts it—focus on smaller facets.

> "There's plenty of material out there, if you break it down into workable segments and then focus on extracting the humor."

You surely have a living room, bedroom, kitchen, and bathroom. Maybe you have a family room, a backyard, a garage, a home office, a studio, a library. To get ideas flowing, you can concentrate on any one of these areas.

What happens in any one of these rooms that might prompt a humorous article? If you think about it hard enough—really focus on it for a while—you'll find that plenty happens. Once again, we're searching for the obvious that we always seem to overlook.

Let's take the bathroom, for example. Nothing funny ever happens there, you might think. But it does. Here's a portion of an article I did based on a very serious problem in my own family bathroom:

> I'm a sincere believer that toothpaste should be squeezed from the end of the tube. My wife is relaxed about toothpaste tube squeezing. She has no agenda, no strategy. She simply picks up the tube and squeezes wherever her grip happens to fall.
>
> My philosophy is that end-of-the-tube squeezing is much quicker, more efficient, and more economical. Also, aesthetically, the tube is much more appealing. My wife's theory is "get some goop on the brush, clean the teeth, and get on with the rest of the day."
>
> Our marriage is a bathroom version of the Hatfields and

McCoys feud. I will dutifully squeeze the paste from the bottom. Then she'll nullify my efforts by squeezing from any old place. Next day, I'll again rectify her error and squeeze from where toothpaste tubes should be squeezed. She'll squeeze from the middle again.

Finally, one day I complained and my wife said, "What's the big deal?"

I said, "What's the big deal? What's the big deal?"

She said, "Yes, that was the original question—'What's the big deal?'"

I said, "Let me explain it to you."

She giggled. No, it was worse than a giggle. She *snickered*.

I said, "Are you laughing at me?"

She said, "I'm sorry, but I'm always amused when you go into your 'tutorial' mode."

I said, "What's so funny about me trying to explain a perfectly logical physical phenomenon to you?"

She said, "I don't know. It's just that whenever you do it's like Pavarotti holding a clinic on pole vaulting."

I asked, "Are you trying to say that I don't know what I'm talking about?"

She said, "No, I'm not *trying* to say that. I think I *just did* say that."

I said, "Well, I'm going to get my point across despite your sarcasm."

I held up a tube of toothpaste.

My wife said, "Oh, this is an illustrated lecture?"

Ignoring that, I said, "You'll notice that after you've used the tube, there is toothpaste gathered at both the bottom and the top of the tube. Now all of that paste at the bottom eventually must be squeezed towards the top, which is what I do daily. It should be obvious that to do that, requires much more work."

My wife said, "That's so *you*."

I said, "What is so *me*?"

She said, "To consider squeezing a dollop of toothpaste onto a brush as work."

I harrumphed. I always do that when I can't think of a comeback.

She went on. "You want to know what work is, try picking up your laundry from around the house. Do that for a couple of days and you'll be too tired to brush your teeth."

I said, "I don't leave my dirty clothes lying around."

She said, "Hah!" She always does that when she can think of a comeback. "Your clothes from yesterday were all over the bedroom this morning. I didn't know if you got changed or if you exploded."

I said, "You're creating a diversionary argument because you're missing my basic point."

She countered, "And you're missing my basic point."

I said, "Which is what?"

She answered, "That I don't give a flying dental floss whether I miss your basic point or not."

So to this day she squeezes her way; I squeeze mine.

I did a similar type of article that resulted from focusing on the bedroom. I like the sheet to extend over the blanket when I sleep. My spouse keeps it under the blanket. Somewhere in the middle there is "turbulence." That became the basis for a humorous article.

The kitchen inspired several pieces. One was me, the husband, trying to find something in the refrigerator. My wife kept telling me to look behind something, but it was never there. By the time my wife asked, "What are you looking for?" I couldn't remember.

Focusing on the kitchen area produced another article called "Shopping in Bulk." It was prompted by the current trend of buying things in larger quantities because they're cheaper at warehouse stores. Again, I was searching for something in the cupboard. (It seems I'm always looking for things in the kitchen. The only thing in the kitchen that I know the location of is the sink. Incidentally, this prompted another article on the premise that wives always know where *everything* is, and husbands know where *nothing* is.) However, the cupboard was loaded with items in *massive* quantities. There was a gallon bottle of vanilla extract; four burlap bags of parsley, sage, rosemary, and thyme; a bushel of honey-roasted peanuts; a box of soap powder that was larger than our guest room; and two sacks of coffee that were thrown over the back of a mule being held in place by Juan Valdez himself.

Another idea that converted nicely to an article was the trouble I had opening things in the kitchen. So many products in the kitchen have instructions for easy opening. The instructions are neither easy, nor do they open anything.

There are plenty of ideas within the four walls of your own home. You can uncover them if you divide and focus.

Chapter Eight

Slant and Approach

You've spent a little bit of time—well, maybe quite a bit of time—focusing on different areas for comedy ideas. You've taken a close look at your own past. You've isolated several topics that you might write about. You've looked at all angles from a time or geographic perspective. You've got that item now that you feel you can write funny about.

Well, your preparatory work is still not done.

Now you have to decide on your *slant* on that topic. The slant is your point of view on that premise. What are you going to say about it? For example, let's say you've decided to write about the proliferation of cell phones. You're investigation has shown that they're everywhere. The driver in the car next to you on the highway is talking on his mobile phone. Maybe the person in the passenger seat is also on a cell phone. Maybe they're talking to each other. Who knows?

Youngsters have cell phones. Soccer moms have cell phones. Business people carry them. A Little League father in the stands can now call his son out in right field and tell him to play this batter closer to the foul line. The Little League manager can call the father's wife and ask her to call her husband to tell him not to be calling the players during the game.

A housewife shopping in aisle three of the supermarket can call her friend who is shopping in aisle seven and gossip about their mutual friend who is shopping in aisle four.

You've decided that there's humor in this subject and you know you can write a funny piece on it. But what stand do you take? Do you hate them because they're so ubiquitous and annoying? Or do you favor them because now you can talk to anyone at anytime from anywhere? Maybe you enjoy your cell phone because you can talk from the privacy of your car during your drive to and from work without having anyone interrupt your conversation. In the office, people will frequently walk in on you while you're on the phone. It's not often they'll do that while you're zipping along the freeway at seventy miles an hour.

You might condemn cell phones and propose that they be banned or you may commend them and wish that they had been around forty or fifty years sooner.

I once wrote an article about the roadrunner not being able to fly. My angle was how silly it was to have a bird, a creature supposedly born to soar, not being able to get off the ground. My article centered on how frustrating and annoying it must be for this animal not being able to lift off.

I might just as easily written a piece on how comforting it might have been for the roadrunner not having to fly. It could have been a tremendous relief not being obliged to fly. He doesn't have to get nudged out of the nest to try his wings. He doesn't have to search for updrafts and downdrafts to control his flight. He doesn't have to expend the energy of feverishly flapping his wings to stay aloft. No. He simply stays on the ground. The animal pecks through the egg shell, emerges into a heartless world, and immediately is retired. That's a pretty doggone easy life for a bird.

Comedian Drew Carey used to do a routine about how terrible it must have been for a person to be in a vegetative state knowing that someone is about to "pull the plug." Drew Carey said that you would probably welcome that…unless…being a vegetable was the greatest thing that ever happened to you.

Whatever point of view you decide on is valid. You can write whatever you want on your premise. There is no wrong or right for a humorist. You're stating a point of view for your reader's enjoyment. As a humorist, you can take either side of any argument or create a whole new perspective and expand on that.

However, it will help your writing if you decide on your approach before you begin your article and then remain consistent with that slant.

There are three areas you might consider before finalizing your slant on your article:

1) What do you think about your premise?

2) What is the traditional thinking about your premise?

3) How does your market feel about this premise?

The first item is probably the most important to your writing. Humor is very subjective. You usually say or write what strikes you as funny. People react to humor according to what they think is funny. Good comedy should be passionate. You should feel strong about what you write about. The best way to do that is to be convinced of your point of view.

During my career as a gag-writer for hire, I obviously worked for different people. Sometimes I would create my own premises and create humor that I felt was suitable to my client's style. At other times, though, the client would call with "assignments." The person I was writing for would supply the topics. It was always easier to write on the things that I created.

It's just simpler to write strongly about something you feel strong about.

However, being aware of the current thinking about your topic, even if you do not agree with it, can help your writing, too—for several reasons.

First, if you know what people are expecting to hear, you can more easily surprise them. Remember, surprise is a major element of humor. A good example of this is the premise I mentioned earlier from Drew Carey. The general consensus is that no one would want to exist as a "vegetable." Carey drew humor from the idea that maybe that might be a great existence. You could be creating your own ecstasy in your dream-like state. It might be like a permanent high. In any case, Carey's comedy came from the fact that he was contradicting the traditional thinking on this subject.

Second, shock is another element of humor, probably because it is surprising. But shock goes a little bit beyond mere surprise. I remember reading a line somewhere about hunting. The author said, "I could never kill an animal like that." For many, that's the traditional thinking. However, the author then added, "No, I like to just wound them." That's a surprise against the tradition thinking, but it's also jarring.

Third—and we're back to research here—if you are aware of the common thinking on your subject, you can now search for ways to confound it. As a humorist, you can purposely explore the other angles. You can be unique in your thinking. You can expose those thoughts on this subject that are obvious, but again, no one ever really thought about. And this thinking doesn't necessarily have to be confrontational. As a short example, consider this angle that Jerry Seinfeld has used in his stand-up routine: Why do skydivers wear helmets? We all have just accepted that skydivers wear protective headgear. No one has ever challenged that. Yet, as Seinfeld points out, what good is a plastic helmet going to do when you fall from 20,000 feet in the air?

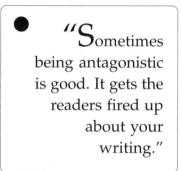

"Sometimes being antagonistic is good. It gets the readers fired up about your writing."

There's a lot of humor to be found in pointing out the silliness of some of our traditional beliefs. You can only explore that silliness if you first know what the traditional beliefs are.

Fourth, maybe you do want to be confrontational. Sometimes being antagonistic is good. It gets the readers fired up about your writing. It gets them involved emotionally. There's a gentleman who writes song parodies for the Rush Limbaugh show. These comedic songs are meant to rile a good portion of the listeners. The Limbaugh followers think the ditties are hilarious. The anti-Rush crowd is upset by them. That means the songs have served their purpose. The writer knows what the other side is thinking and purposely writes parodies that attack that point of view.

The third aspect is important in writing humorous articles for sale, or in deciding which periodicals you will offer your writing to. For instance, using the above example, you would certainly not write a song parody criticizing liberal politics and offer it to Al Franken's radio show. Rush Limbaugh will buy it, but Al Franken won't.

I once sold several humorous pieces to a woman's magazine. They liked my writing style and were purchasing regularly from me. Then I sent them one funny piece that was rejected quickly. I was surprised because I felt this article was as funny or funnier than many of the one's they published. On reflection, and on rereading the article, I saw the light. In all of my other pieces about domestic situations, I played the fall guy. I, as the husband, the father, or the grandfather, was the one that the laughs were on. In this particular piece, though, I kidded some idiosyncrasy of my fictional spouse. I was, in effect, making fun of the woman. That's not too wise for a woman's magazine. They rejected this piece because it was wrong for their readers.

This doesn't mean that you have to sell out your point of view and become a charlatan who writes only what the people want to hear. You can still adhere to point number one and put on paper whatever you feel about your particular premise. But it does mean, then, that certain publications will not want to publish your particular point of view.

However, another publication might.

It also means, though, that you might want to temper your comments on certain subjects. Often you might be able to form your thoughts so that they are acceptable to certain readers.

That leads us to the next part of this chapter—the approach you take in your article.

How to say it

Now that you know what you're going to write about and what you want to say about it, you must decide on how you're going to say it. This can often be the heart of your humor. This can be where your creativity shines. Here's where your humor can become unique and inventive.

In coaching gag writers I would often recommend that they say something by not saying it. I realize that sounds oxymoronic. Many of my students would even suggest dropping the "oxy" from that evaluation. But jokes where you can *imply* the humor rather than saying it outright are usually more powerful. They force the listeners to think. The punch line not only comes as more of a surprise and thus has more of a jolt to it, but the audience is involved. They almost have to write their own punch line.

Here are a few one-liners that illustrate this point:

Rodney Dangerfield says in his act,

My father gave me a bat for Christmas. First time I tried to play with it, it flew away.

That's a fantastic joke. Notice how much stronger it is in that form than it would be if he came right out and expressed his humor.

My father gave me a bat for Christmas. Oh, I don't mean the kind you play baseball with. I mean the kind that hangs upside down in a cave.

Good joke. The comedy idea is there, but it's much more powerful when he *says it by not saying it.*

Some comic once said,

The nice thing about old age—you can whistle while you brush your teeth.

That's a much more powerful joke than if the comic said,

Old age isn't so bad. I still have all my teeth. I keep them in a glass by my bed.

Bob Hope used to kid his golfing buddy, Jerry Ford. Ford was famous for hitting bystanders when he played golf. Hope could have said,

Jerry Ford is a dangerous golfer. Every time he hits the ball, he hits a person, too.

It's a rather direct way of stating the gag. Instead of that, Hope said,

> **It's easy to spot Jerry Ford on the golf course. He has the only golf cart with a red cross on top.**

Notice, in this version Hope never mentions the fact that Ford hits people. He implies it pretty forcefully, though.

This same device applies in writing humorous articles, also. Perhaps you can make your comedic point by not mentioning your point at all. Let your readers figure it out for you.

Here's an article that I wrote kidding myself as a writer, and I believe kidding a lot of other writers, too. Many of us avoid the keyboard any way we can. We mean well, but we always find some way of postponing our tasks. This short article makes that point, but it never mentions procrastination.

The Great American Novel (to come)

America is a glorious country. Home of the free and land of the brave. She is a nation who certainly deserves a great novel. Mark Twain has written some fair ones. Hemingway, Faulkner, Fitzgerald, Jones, Mailer, Capote—they did some O.K. work, too. *Gone With the Wind* enjoyed a modicum of success. But still, the Great American Novel has not been written...until now.

I feel ordained to write it. I'm certainly qualified. American born and raised. I've read most of the current best-selling novels and a few of the classics. I've attended many writing seminars and I own my own computer.

It should have some heft to it, probably about 120,000 words. At 1,000 words a day, with weekends off, the Great American Novel is only twenty-four weeks away from completed manuscript form.

Certainly, writing the Great American Novel will bring me fame. I'll be gracious to Donahue and Oprah, patient with Geraldo, and I'll treat both Regis and Kathie Lee as equals. It'll make me rich, too, but the celebrity and wealth are trivial perks, more to be endured than savored. What's important is the Work.

What it will be about I don't yet know, but I believe that the inspiration will come from above, as did the holy commission. I must write this epic. I must write it now.

But first…

I have pencils to sharpen.

"You've been sharpening pencils for about an hour and a half now," my wife says. "What is it you don't want to write now?"

I said, "I don't *want* to write anything, but I'm *compelled* to write the Great American Novel."

"And even though you have a state of the art computer that has a CD player that shows pictures of the Hindenburg disaster, you still have to sharpen seven dozen pencils before you can begin?"

Perhaps my novel will be about a creative genius who manages to produce scintillating work despite the sarcasm of his spouse.

"Yes," I say, "I do. Pointy pencils are the symbol of fine literature. They are inspiration to the scribe. They say that Shakespeare could not even begin a playlet without a mugful of sharpened pencils on his writing desk."

"I don't think pencils were invented when Shakespeare was alive," she says.

"No?" I say.

"No," she says.

"Well, all the more pity," I say. "Think what he might have produced had he had them. I do have them and I'm going to avail myself of their motivation."

She says, "Fine. Do you want something to eat or are you going to sharpen through lunch?"

I tell her, "I can't think of food now. I have the Great American Novel to write."

But first…

"What are you doing now?" my wife asks.

"I'm writing the Great American Novel."

"With a vacuum cleaner?"

"This is all part and parcel of the process," I explain. "Necessary chores for the one selected to write the Great American Novel."

"To vacuum the rug?"

"Absolutely. First of all, I can't think imaginatively in a dust-tainted ambiance. Second, years from now tourists will flock here to see the room where the Great American Novel was born. You and I don't want them to stand behind the red velvet guide ropes and think to themselves: how could he be so incredibly ingenious amid so many dust balls and cobwebs?"

She said, "I wouldn't want them to think that."

"Nor I," I said. "So please leave and let me finish my vacuuming so I can get started on the Great American Novel."

She left and I was ready to start.

But first…

"Darling," I yelled to my wife.

"Yes?" she hollered back.

"What's your Aunt Gert's husband's name?"

"Philo. Uncle Philo."

"How do you spell it?"

"P-H-I-L-O. Why do you want to know?"

"Because I hate to misspell a person's name."

"No, I mean why do you want to know Aunt Gert's husband's name?"

"Oh. Because I'm making a list of people I want to send autographed copies of my novel to."

My wife came into my office. This confrontation had to be face to face. "You're making a list of people you want to send autographed copies of your book to?"

"Yes," I said.

She said, "But you haven't written anything yet."

She just didn't understand. "This book," I said, "is going to take the country by storm. The demands on my time will be unbelievable. If I don't get this done now, I'll never get it done and it's your relatives who are going to be offended."

She left without another word.

I got back to my list and to the beginning of my Great American Novel.

But first…

I gathered up some pens, notepads, a thesaurus, my sunglasses and ambled through the family room towards the back patio.

"Where are you going now?" my wife asked.

"Outside," I said.

"What for?"

"To work."

She said, "Your sharpened pencils, clean rug, and list of distant relatives are in your office. Why are you going outside?"

"There's inspiration in fresh air," I said. "Do you know who wrote outdoors?"

My wife said, "Gaugin."

I said, "He was an artist, not a writer."

My wife said, "No, he was a writer. He just did that painting thing to get himself in the mood to write the Great Tahitian Novel."

"I'll be outside," I said, "working on my novel."

I went outside to work on my novel.

But first…

I fixed a water sprinkler that had been leaking for some time, and I straightened the bird bath because it was listing badly, then I took a few practice golf swings because creative writing is hard work and I needed relaxation.

Then my wife spoiled the mood. "Dinner's ready," she said.

I thought about working through the evening meal but it wouldn't be fair to my project. Even literary geniuses require sustenance, and a novel of the proportions I envisioned would demand my full strength.

I ate, had a cup of coffee, then yawned and said, "I'm going to take a warm bath and get to bed early."

My wife said, "Tomorrow are you actually going to do some writing?"

"Of course, I am," I said. "As Hugh Prather once wrote, 'If the desire to write is not accompanied by actual writing then the desire is not to write.'"

"Hugh Prather wrote that?" she asked.

"Yes, he did," I said.

My wife said, "That's profound. I wonder how many pencils he had to sharpen before he wrote that? How long he vacuumed the carpet? How long his list of relatives was. How many sprinklers and bird baths..."

My wife's mumbling trailed off as I left and headed for my bath and bed. No need for me to remain and be made sport of. I had to get up in the morning and begin work on the Great American Novel. I was already behind.

You might also use a "what if" device to present your humor. For instance, in talking about cell phones you might wonder what if the American Indian had had cell smoke signals? In restaurants they might have started a small fire on the table and sent messages to their friends. While driving along the highway, they could have started a fire in the passenger side of the car and began transmitting smoke signals.

You might extend your premise out to its bizarre conclusion. If the proliferation of cell phones continues, what will life be like 2,000 years from now? Will we be making cell phone calls from other planets? Will we be able to place collect calls to distant stars?

Sometimes the humor of your piece will be entirely dependent on the way you present your premise. The ways to approach your presentation are limited only by your creativity. If you invent a new approach and it gets your idea across comedically, use it. But as with the slant, it will help your writing if you decide on your approach before attacking the article.

Chapter Nine

Basic Structure of a Humorous Article

The nice part of humor is that it's mischievous. It likes to misbehave. It enjoys breaking the rules. A major element of any good punch line is "surprise." Bob Hope used to read some of the material we writers would hand to him and he'd look at us and say, "Where's the surprise? Where's the twist?"

To get a reaction from an audience or readers, you must catch them unaware. Your comedy has to be unpredictable.

So, by all means, if you have a unique, funny, unpredictable way of presenting your humor, do it. Rules fall by the wayside when you're getting guffaws.

Nevertheless, there is a traditional structure to most writing and until you can find an inventive and effective way of violating the code, it would be well to be aware of it and conform to it in at least some of your humor writing.

As with all story telling, your tale must have a beginning, a middle, and an end. That is something to get them interested in the tale, something to keep them interested, and then something to justify the time they spent with this story by resolving it.

Let's take the story of Cinderella as an example. It needs a beginning, obviously, because you have to get the story started. And at the beginning you have to learn a bit about your characters. Cinderella is a lovely young lady who is sadly mistreated by her unattractive and not too personable stepsisters and by her spiteful stepmother. We know who we're dealing with now. We know who to root for and who to root against.

But suppose we leave out the middle. The prince has a wonderful ball, but Cinderella's mean old step relatives don't want her to go. So, she doesn't.

Pretty dull story, isn't it?

Fortunately, the story does have a middle. The Fairy Godmother steps in to add some dimension to this drama. She outfits Cinderella in a beautiful gown and provides an elegant carriage and distinguished coachmen to take her to the event. However, the spell only lasts until midnight. This Fairy Godmother must get her powers from a rental shop that has strict return rules.

Imagine, though, that the story had no end. Cinderella goes to the ball, has a few sips of punch, dances a waltz or two, then goes home and starts cleaning out the hearth again.

Still not much of a tale, is it?

Fortunately, the writer gave us a clever denouement. In her rush to get back to her house before midnight, Cinderella loses a glass slipper. The prince searches for the only dainty foot in the kingdom that will fit it. He finds Cinderella, marries her, and they live happily ever after.

Beginning, middle, and end.

Even jokes, probably the most concise form of story telling, have a similar structure. As an example, let's look at one of my favorite Bob Hope jokes. Here again he was talking about his buddy Jerry Ford.

I enjoy playing golf with Jerry Ford. You never have to keep score when you play with him. You just look back along the fairway and count the wounded.

The beginning tells you he's talking about golf with his friend, President Ford. The middle, though, throws a little drama into it. Wait a minute, you enjoy playing with such a wild golfer? And how come you don't have to keep score? Then the ending resolves it. You don't have to keep score because for every shot he's taken, there's a wounded body lying along the course.

Beginning, middle, and end

Your short humor should also follow this tradition.

The beginning should accomplish several things. It should set your premise. Tell the readers what your piece is about. However, it should do this in a compelling way. It should be informative, but it should also be intriguing. The reader should glance over your first few sentences and want to read on. If they don't read on, the best comedy in the world won't score.

You want to start strong. Phyllis Diller once confessed to me why she wore bizarre costumes in her act. "When I first walk on stage," she said, "I want to do a strong joke. I want to let the people know I'm funny. So I wore these crazy costumes which would get a laugh, and then I could do a joke about the costume." She would get her big laugh and then move on to the rest of her act.

In a humorous article, you don't have to start with a big laugh, but you do have to start strong. A laugh is fine if you can get one quickly. If not, though, you need something to capture the reader—keep him reading until he gets to the laughs.

The middle of your piece, of course, now delivers on the promise of that solid beginning. Here's where you deliver the clever irony, the smart repartee, the inventive observations. Here's where you get a chance to show your real genius. Have fun with it.

The ending should satisfy the readers. They should get the feeling that they've read a complete piece and are happy with the way you treated it. The ending doesn't have to be as powerful and compelling as the opening, but it should be strong enough to leave the readers content.

Unsatisfying endings are…well, unsatisfying. One editor told me that it's like watching a classic mystery story. At the end the detective calls all of the suspects into one room and then tells them, "I don't know what happened in this case."

That's disappointing. No, you want the detective to point by point resolve the mystery.

There are several ways to end your humorous articles. One way is to simply end them. Go as far as you can with the humor…and *stop*. That's it. End of article. If you recall the old "Monty Python" shows and films, they would often do this. They'd have an hilariously funny sketch on a bizarre premise and when they were done with it, they'd simply have an announcer say, "And now for something completely different." They'd go on to the next funny bit. That worked for them because it was zany. Remember we did say that humor has no hard and fast rules. Breaking what rules we do have can even add to the humor.

In print, though, this gimmick is usually not very well received.

You can also end a sketch by beginning it again, or looking forward to what might happen in the future. For instance, suppose I have a sketch that begins with a gentleman coming up to me on the street and saying, "Hey buddy, would you like to buy a watch?" The guy is a persistent salesman and nothing I do can free me from his tactics. It leads to some funny sights and sounds. Finally, through some ploy I get rid of him. The ending of the article might be another street salesman coming up to me and saying, "Hey buddy, you want to buy a ring?"

> "Remember we did say that humor has no hard and fast rules. Breaking what rules we do have can even add to the humor."

It loops back and leaves the reader feeling that the whole farce is going to start over again. With the right premise it can be a worthwhile ending. It does refer back to the start of the piece and ties the whole thing in a nice little knot.

Probably the most effective ending is to refer back to the beginning of your article. Take the premise you started with and comment on it as your ending. It terminates the work for the reader.

The previous ending device does refer back to the beginning but it leaves the reader with some work to do. The reader either has to mentally write a whole new article or has to guess at what is going to happen next. With this style of ending, the article is indeed complete. As an example of this type of ending, I once did an article that began with a bit of trivia in the newspaper that said that roadrunners cannot fly. The middle of the piece was several different thoughts on how silly it was to have a flightless bird. It's like having a flightless airplane. Birds are made to fly; so are airplanes. Imagine getting to the airport, going through security, checking your luggage, fighting the crowd at the boarding gate, settling into your seat, fastening your seatbelt, and having the pilot say, "I'm sorry, ladies and gentlemen, but this is a flightless airplane…" You get the idea of what the column was like.

Towards the ending, I checked the encyclopedia which told me that roadrunners can fly, they simply choose not to. I ended the article by saying, "Forget everything I just said…oh, and don't believe everything you read in the newspaper."

Choose one topic

I got some advice from an editor when I first began writing humor pieces for magazines.

First, he advised that short, humorous pieces work best when they are on one subject. Select a premise and stick with it from top to bottom. Of course, you can introduce various aspects of that one premise, but stay on the main topic.

I asked why. He said because humor has to build. It has to be set up. Earlier I told you about Ed Sullivan asking Phyllis Diller to cut all the non-funny lines from her act for his show. The non-funny lines were the ones that set up the funny lines. Without the straight lines there could be no punch line.

So in short pieces, it's more effective to set the topic up once and then have fun with it. If a writer keeps switching to different topics, the readers have to readjust. They have to stop and re-start. It's confusing.

Also, with written pieces the writer doesn't have the luxury of unlimited time or space. It's sometimes difficult to develop a premise, have fun with it, and resolve it in the space of 750 to 800 words. It's that much more difficult to go through the same procedure with three, four, or five different premises in the same limited word count.

Stand-up comedians can sometimes switch from premise to premise easily because they are orchestrating the audience. Also, the spoken word doesn't require as much time for transitions as the written piece does.

So explore your topic as fully as you can. If you have other topics that are funny, maybe they're the beginning of another humorous article.

The other advice he offered we've already discussed—have the ending of the article loop back in some way to the beginning.

One other point that is worth mentioning even though it doesn't strictly deal with the structure of the article, is that it often takes quite a bit of time for the material to leave your typewriter or printer and reach the readers. Magazines have long lead times and sometimes the pieces you write can be backlogged—filed away for future use.

Consequently, it's difficult to be too topical. The reference you use today may be dated by the time your comedy sees the newsstands. Be careful of current references unless you're relatively positive that name or reference will stay in the public's consciousness.

Chapter Ten

How to Begin Writing the Humorous Article

There are probably as many different writing procedures as there are writers. Each writer has his or her own unique work protocol. Some prefer writing in longhand on a ruled pad. Others use tape recorders. Many prefer to sit at a computer keyboard. Some writers still prefer typewriters and a few holdouts even insist on a manual typewriter. I remember a bunch of writers once walked into another writer's office. There on the desk was an old-fashioned manual typewriter.

One of the visiting writers looked at it in disbelief. "How do you plug it in?" he asked.

The owner said, "You don't have to plug it in. You just type on it."

The disbelieving writer exclaimed, "Wow…what won't they think of next?"

I prefer to use a keyboard of some sort—computer or typewriter. For me, it's not really a preference but a necessity. When I was writing one-liners for comics and television shows, I would think for some time on the subject and then the jokes would start to flow into my head. When they came, they came quickly. I would try to keep up with them with my handwriting, but the jokes would get ahead of me. Consequently, my handwriting became illegible. Sometimes, because of circumstances, I would be forced to write out my material in longhand anyway. If I did not transcribe those jokes the same day, while they were still fresh in my mind, I would often find later that I couldn't read my own writing.

Longhand for me was not the best option.

However, some writers prefer writing their material out for just the opposite, but just as valid, reason. Forming each letter of each word slows them down enough so they can really think out what they're writing.

Which way is right? Whichever one works for the individual writer.

Some writers must work from an outline. It gives them a road map to the entire project their working on. It helps them keep their thoughts focused in the right direction. Others enjoy the freedom of creating as they go. An outline hampers their creativity.

Again, the right way is the way that works.

I like to have an ending in mind for any teleplay or short piece that I write. It gives me confidence that the project is doable. It also gives my writing direction. Anything I put into that piece should be directed toward that ending. For me it gives drive and pace to the writing.

I remember one time, however, when I violated my own rule. My partner and I were working on a comedy script for a situation comedy. We had sold the producers on a general premise and they gave us a go-ahead for the teleplay.

> "There are probably as many different writing procedures as there are writers."

My partner and I crafted the first several scenes of the story, but were having trouble coming up with a suitable resolution. We hadn't planned the ending beforehand. We kept delaying finishing the script because frankly we didn't know how it would finish. We had painted ourselves into a corner.

One day, at our desks, we resolved to stay at the typewriter until we pounded out the final scene and delivered it to the producers. We not only wanted to get done, but we wanted our paychecks. Finishing the script was the only way of getting them.

So, with enough coffee on hand to see us through this ordeal, we put blank paper into the typewriter and typed in the heading and location for the final scene.

Before we could put one well-written word on the paper, the phone rang. It was the producers of the show.

"Put whatever you've got into an envelope and deliver it to our office immediately," they said.

"But we're not finished with it yet," we informed them. They said,

"It doesn't matter. Get whatever you have to us now so we can pay you. The show's been canceled, effective immediately."

We gave them the unfinished script, collected our money, and to this day we have no idea how that story would end.

That's one reason why I always like to have at least a general idea of the resolution before beginning any writing project. Yet I know very effective writers who are just as adamant about not having an ending in mind. They claim that they bring more enthusiasm to the writing when they're not exactly sure where the story or the article is going.

Again, I recall two writers on *The Carol Burnett Show* who felt an ending was imperative before beginning a project. The producer was after them for a sketch but they kept delaying it. Finally, the producer called these writers in for a meeting. In no uncertain terms he told them that he needed this sketch quickly.

They said, "Well, we're having trouble finding an appropriate ending and we can't really write the sketch until we know how it's going to end."

The producer said, "You want an ending? I'll give you an ending. Tim Conway falls out a window. Now have the sketch on my desk end of day tomorrow."

There are some writing protocols I won't recommend. I was head writer on one variety show writing staff and I had a sketch that needed some punching up. The writing partners working in the office next to mine were very good at writing the type of comedy I needed. I thought I'd just pop in and pick their brains for a bit.

I opened the door and walked in. One of the partners was seated at his desk doing the typing. The other was pacing back and forth, dictating material. He was puffing on a large Churchill cigar and he wore a derby hat. He wore nothing else.

As I said, I don't recommend this writing procedure. I also don't recommend ever walking in on these two writers without knocking.

There is no strict set of rules for any kind of writing. You 're not obliged to start with step number one then move on to step two, and so on. You can if you want to, but only if you want to and even then only if it produces quality results. The purpose of professional writing is to produce professional writing. People want to read what you write; they don't care how you wrote it. Whatever gets your thoughts on paper is the method you should use.

With that said, I'd like to walk through a system that I most often use to write humorous articles. It is only a system; it's not a statute. It usually works for me and by outlining it here, you might discover that it works for you. Or you might find that parts of it work for you. Fine… take from it what is beneficial. Perhaps in reading it over, you'll discover ways to improve the method that you use presently. Or you may decide that your way is better than this. That's fine. Whatever gets it on paper for you is the formula you should use.

My process

Let me take you through an actual process in order to illustrate my method. I'll use as an example an article I wrote when I first began doing the humor column for *Arizona Highways*. I called the piece "There's Gold in Them Hills." When it appeared in the magazine, the editors had retitled it "Maybe What It Takes to Find the Dutchman's Lost Gold Is a Helpful Wife."

1) I began by focusing on some area in order to find a premise that I could write about. Since I was working for a regional magazine, focusing geographically seemed logical. Now that's not always imperative. Sometimes I can get a family oriented topic that I want to write about—for instance, my own forgetfulness—and then find a way to tie that in someway to Arizona.

In this case, though, I did focus on geography. One of the more well-known tales about the Superstition Mountains in Arizona is the legend of the Lost Dutchman's Gold Mine. I read about this and discovered that a prospector named Don Miguel Peralta uncovered a generous gold mine in 1845. However, he and his miners were ambushed and killed by Apache Indians. One survivor later revealed the location to a German immigrant named Jacob Waltz, known as the "Dutchman." Waltz worked the mine, made a fortune, but never revealed its whereabouts. After his death, countless prospectors searched for this rich vein, but they either got hopelessly lost in the mountains or were later found murdered. No rich gold deposits have ever been found in the general area and experts claim that it's not a likely location for gold, yet the legend endures to this day.

With this background material, I decided that I would search for and find the Lost Dutchman's Gold Mine.

2) The slant I decided on was that I would wake up one morning and decide that my goal in life was to find this mine. Of course, my wife would accept that boast with much spousal skepticism.

3) Now I let the idea "marinate." I get a concept that I like and feel I can write effectively, then I avoid working on it for maybe a day or two days. My idea is that even though I'm not consciously thinking about the article, subconsciously I am. Of course, if a random thought about the piece pops into my head and seems to have value, I'll make a note of it.

I feel strongly about this part of my own writing procedure. I also think it adds a lot of fun to the creative process. Once I was given a quite generous assignment. It was an idea that I liked and was enthusiastic about writing it. Then the editor handed me a story outline. I told him I preferred to write my own. He said, "No, you must write this one. It's already been approved." I turned down the assignment. If I can't think about the topic and generate my own ideas about it, then I can't really write it effectively.

4) I'll lay out the idea in broad strokes. In this case, I decided that I would search for the mine and my wife would object to my bizarre endeavor. She would be skeptical, but I would be insistent. At the end, I would hardly be able to get out of the house because I could never find anything in the house—my shoes, my jacket, my car keys. To me, this felt like a plausible ending.

5) Then I got into the actual writing. I believe that the joke is the

basic building block of humor. A monologue, obviously, is a series of jokes strung together in logical form. To me, a humorous article is similar. Now, "joke" may be a limiting term in this situation. Some writers object to thinking in terms of "jokes." However, I'm using the word "joke" to express any funny concept that might go into the article. It might be a piece of dialogue. It might be an irony. It might just be a clever use of words.

In any case, I begin by just thinking about humorous concepts... in no particular order. If I can come up with something amusing about my topic, I'll jot it down.

Now this is a concerted effort. It's focusing again. I'm looking into the topic to try to uncover the fun in it. Ironically, I'm trying to mine the humor in the Lost Dutchman's Mine.

Although I like to write at a keyboard, this step for me is more relaxed. I'll sit in a comfortable chair, often outside, and just think about the topic. When a "joke" hits, I jot it down. (Of course, for reasons I mentioned earlier, I immediately take these notes to the keyboard and transcribe them into readable form.)

Here are just a few ideas that I generated in this working session:

I had an idea that my wife would object to the expense. I jotted down dialogue like this:

> **Spouse: How much is this going to cost?**
> **Me: Not much. How much can it cost to wander through the desert looking for gold?**
> **Spouse: You're going to need at least one other jackass.**

Then I thought she would be worried about my safety:

> **Spouse: People have died looking for this treasure.**
> **Me: Greed killed those people. They figured the world owed them a living. I'm not that greedy. I figure just Arizona does.**

I thought my wife might wonder where I got such an idea. That prompted this exchange:

Spouse: Where did you ever get such an idea?

Me: I watched a documentary on television about this mine. All during the show I heard this voice saying, "You're going to find this mine. You're going to find this mine." It was the Dutchman talking to me.

Spouse: All during his life he never talked. Now that he's dead, he has a chat with you?

6) Once I gathered enough "chunks" of humor, I begin to arrange them in a logical order and begin to form the sequence of the article. After I've transcribed my notes, still in random order, I'll place numbers in the margin indicating where they should appear in the final writing.

7) Now I begin the writing. The first step is to write an effective lead that states the premise and gets me into the body of the piece.

Then I start following the sequence I've outlined in the notes. Having the sequence arranged allows me to write transitions as I go, and perhaps adding a bit more humor in the process. Of course, I'll sometimes alter the sequence during the writing, but the original sequencing at least gets me started.

Also, during this writing, I can see where new jokes might be needed. Perhaps the transition is too abrupt in certain places. Often, too, I'll discover that one "joke" in my notes may contradict another one. If the two are not compatible, I'll either have to change one or the other, or perhaps drop one "chunk" entirely or replace it with a new concept. The original outline and notes serve only as a road map. The writing itself should be creative, inventive.

8) That finishes the writing…but not quite. Again, I like to let the piece "marinate." I'll type out the entire piece and set it aside, possibly for a day or two. Then I'll resurrect the article and read through it, making corrections, additions, and deletions as I go.

I like to allow a few days before the rewrite because I find if I do it too soon after the actual writing, I don't view it with a fair perspective.

I'm still too close to the creative process. After some time has elapsed, I can read through it more objectively.

9) Then, of course, I retype the whole thing and send it off to the editor—or in some cases, to the trash can.

Following is the final result of my work on the Lost Dutchman's Mine:

There's Gold in Them Hills

Have you ever had one of those mornings when you wake up and the sun seems brighter, the air smells fresher, and colors are much more vibrant? That's the way this morning was for me. I went to breakfast full of enthusiasm, knowing all was right with the world.

"I know how I'm going to make my fortune," I told my wife.

"For a man in his late fifties that's commendable," she said.

Well, almost all was right with the world.

I didn't let her negativity affect me. "I'm going to find the Lost Dutchman's Mine," I announced.

"I see," she said, somewhat patronizingly as she scraped the black crust from some burnt toast. "And where exactly is this Lost Dutchman's Mine?"

She was trying to trick me, but I wouldn't fall for it. "Well, no one knows exactly where it is; otherwise it wouldn't be lost, would it? But it's somewhere in the Superstition Mountains."

"And so are the bones of a lot of the people who tried to find it."

"That's all right," I said. "Less competition."

"People can die from looking for lost treasures," she said.

I defended my position, though. "Greed killed those people. They figured the world owed them a living. I'm not that greedy. I figure just Arizona does."

"Where'd you get this idea?" she asked as two more burnt pieces of bread popped up.

"I watched a documentary last night about this lost gold mine and all during the show I kept hearing 'You're the man who's going to find it, you're the man who's going to find it.' It was like the Dutchman was talking to me."

My wife was unimpressed. "All during his life he never talked. Now that he's dead he has a chat with you?"

"Well, he didn't actually talk to me," I said. "I just know that if I go looking for the mine, I'll find it. I've always considered myself lucky. I married you, didn't I?" A little soft soap, I figured, wouldn't hurt.

My wife said, "I've sometimes considered myself unlucky for the same reason."

The soft soap didn't help, either.

"Look, honey," I said. "I have this feeling. This lost gold mine is just sitting out there and if I can find it we'll be rich. You'll have a maid to do the dishes. We'll go everywhere by chauffeur driven limousine. I'll even get you a toaster that works."

"Which brings up an interesting point. How much is this going to cost?"

I felt I almost had her convinced. "Not much. Maybe a few supplies, that's all."

She said, "You're going to need at least one other jackass."

Apparently I hadn't convinced her.

She said, "Suppose you do find this gold mine. You don't know anything about gold."

"That true," I admitted. "But I've always been fond of it."

"Do you know how to spot gold in the ground?"

"No."

"Do you know how to mine it, load it in carts, and bring it to the surface?"

"No, not really."

"Do you know how to extract the gold and refine it?"

"No."

"Do you know that no rich gold deposits have ever been found in the Superstition Mountains, and geologists, naturalists, and engineers all agree that it's an unlikely location for gold?"

"C'mon. What do they know?"

"You're determined to try this, aren't you?" she asked.

"Honey, it's a dream," I said. " A fantasy. It's a gamble, sure, but every once in a while a man has to chase a rainbow."

"Go chase your rainbow," she said. "But try to keep the costs down. We can't afford to waste money."

"That's my girl." I kissed her and rushed to get dressed. I was eager to get underway. I was going to be the man to find the legendary Lost Dutchman's Gold Mine.

After I washed and dressed, I was going to go shopping for a few things I'd need. "Honey, where are my tennis shoes?"

"In the family room where you took them off," she answered.

They were there.

"Have you seen my hat?"

"It's in the hall closet," she answered patiently.

"My jacket?"

"It's here in the kitchen, over the back of the chair."

"Thanks," I said, and kissed her and rushed out the door.

I came back in.

Without my even asking, she said, "Your car keys are on the credenza in the foyer."

I picked them up and started out the door again. Before I left, though, I heard my wife mutter to herself, "Rest in peace, Dutchman. Your secret is safe."

PART II

Types of
Humorous Articles
and Tips on
Writing Them

Chapter Eleven

Monologue

One of the most acclaimed print humorists of all time was Peter Finley Dunne, who lived from 1867 to 1936. Dunne was a sports columnist and an editor of several newspapers and magazines, but he was best known for his syndicated humor column.

This column featured Mr. Dooley, a Chicago saloon keeper who spoke with a heavy Irish brogue. He would spout his homespun philosophy about "ivrything" that was featured in the newspaper, usually to a regular customer named "Hinnissey." Mr. Dooley noted, "Th' newspaper does ivrything for us. It runs th' polis force an' th' banks, commands th' milishy, controls th' legislachure, baptizes th' young, marries th' foolish, comforts th' afflicted, afflicts the comfortable, buries th' dead an' roasts thim aftherward."

The nationally syndicated, well-read column made Peter Finley Dunne a celebrity and won him plaudits from politicians and presidents and friendship with notables such as Mark Twain and Theodore Roosevelt.

Collections of many of Peter Finley Dunne's columns are still available in book form today, along with several biographies of the author.

I mention his achievements because this is a form of humor writing that one doesn't normally see in today's newspapers or magazines. Yet, it was eminently popular in its time. Perhaps that style is due for a resurrection.

Also, it shows once again that humor is unpredictable. In fact, once comedy becomes predictable, it loses much of its appeal. Therefore, *any* style of humor writing is acceptable...provided it's done well, and it's *funny*.

With that in mind, let's take a look at some of the current forms of humor writing.

The monologue form of humorous article is a series of one-liners, quips, or jokes on a given topic, tied together in a logical flow. It's pretty much the same as you would hear a stand-up comic deliver in a club or what Jay Leno and David Letterman do each night on their respective late night talk shows.

Will Rogers wrote a newspaper column for several years that was mostly in this monologue style. It was quite popular and many of the Will Rogers lines still quoted today are from his column.

I remember one written while Rogers was visiting France. He said that he was in a town called Nice. It's spelled "Nice," but it's pronounced "Neese." Will Rogers said, "The French don't have a word for 'nice.'"

Bob Hope, too, wrote a newspaper column for many years. It was usually a short monologue about his travels or current events.

Erma Bombeck gained prominence as a witty newspaper columnist with this form of column, usually based on her family life.

I grew up in Philadelphia and remember a humorist named Ollie Crawford who wrote a monologue column for the *Philadelphia Inquirer* called "Headline Hopping." I was a big fan of Ollie Crawford's "Headline Hopping." I would not only read it faithfully each morning, but I would clip the columns from the front page and file them in an index box for future reference. I don't have any of them today and have had very little luck in researching Ollie Crawford and his "Headline Hopping" columns.

I can recall only one joke. It has probably remained with me because it was such a terrible pun about a little known news item. Crawford would sometimes comment on major news stories, but just as often would do his gags about some remote item that came over the news wires. This particular column was about a news release that claimed that beer drinking in Germany was on the decline. The Ollie Crawford gag I recall read, "They tried Der Fuehrer; now they're trying Der Fewer."

Headline Hopping was a small section of the front page—maybe three column inches—that was devoted to whimsy, a light-hearted look at the news. It must have been a popular feature—although I can't back this up with statistics—because it was featured on the front page of the *Inquirer* for many years.

As I said, I was a big fan. I wanted to be the next Ollie Crawford. Years later I became an Ollie Crawford imitator, not for the *Philadelphia Inquirer* but for some small weekly suburban newspapers. I wrote on strictly local topics and the column was presented in a box on the front page, just like Crawford's was.

While writing one of these columns, I realized how powerful humor can sometimes be. There was a large pothole in the intersection of two major streets in this community. There was quite a political squabble about who was responsible for its repair and the accompanying costs. Consequently, nothing was done about the pothole.

I wrote a humorous column about that offending hole in the street. Several of the lines were quoted by citizens at a city commissioners meeting. Within a week or two the pothole was repaired.

It was partly because of my humorous monologues in several papers that I landed contracts writing for comedians, then television, finally becoming Bob Hope's head gag-writer.

I remain a devoted and grateful fan of this type of humor writing.

Monologue columns of this type are not nearly as popular as they once were. Editors today, it seems, don't want to sacrifice precious newspaper space with trivia such as humor. Occasionally you'll see humor pieces on the editorial page, but even those are usually not in the monologue style.

Nevertheless, I still feel there is a market for this type of column in both magazines and newspapers. Admittedly, though, it may require some excellent writing, research, and salesmanship to convince editors.

The most receptive avenue would probably be with local papers or regional magazines or community magazines. A creative writer who is familiar with the area can localize the humor, whereas national writers can't. The local writer knows the topics that are being discussed by the residents. He or she knows the people and would probably have a good feel for the thoughts of the readers. Therefore, that writer can be more incisive. The gags can be right on the nose.

We noted earlier that comedy is popular. People do talk about what Leno and Letterman said the night before. That, of course, is on a national level. A good local humorist can accomplish the same thing with a crisp humor column. There's a good chance that you might convince an editor that your column would be quoted around the water coolers in your town, too. That local editor might be interested in a column that would generate readership and reader interest.

Following is an example of the monologue form of humorous column. By way of background, this was written for a column I did for a suburban Philadelphia newspaper. It was called "Perret-Scope." (I told you I was an Ollie Crawford wannabe.) Philadelphia at this time had recently completed a highway called the Schuylkill (Skoo-kul) Expressway. It was controversial project and by the time it was finally completed many considered it unsafe.

...I had a pleasant drive on the Schuylkill Expressway today. Pleasant drive on the Schuylkill Expressway—that means you finish in the same car you started with.

...That road takes you from South Philadelphia to Valley Forge in 25 minutes flat...whether you want to go or not.

...Schuylkill Expressway—that's an old Indian term meaning, "White man drive with forked steering wheel."

...I can always tell when I'm approaching the Schuylkill Expressway. My St. Christopher statue gets down from the dashboard and climbs into the glove compartment.

...It's the only road in the world that you can travel on from one end to the other without once leaving the scene of the accident.

...Actually, our Schuylkill Expressway has been cited by religious leaders all over the world. It ranks second to foxholes as a cure for atheism.

...Some of the potholes on there are big enough to be fox-holes anyway.

...One good thing is you get very few tickets on the Schuylkill Expressway. The reason is the police are afraid to drive on it.

Tips on writing the monologue form

Select your topic and your slant. You can see from the above example that my topic was the Schuylkill Expressway and my approach was that it was an unsafe, treacherous road.

Gather references. Make a list of possible references you can use in your gag writing. These are people, places, things, events, and phrases that may in some way be related to your topic. Often they can be related by being so wildly opposite.

Most one-liners are two or more ideas that are tied together in a unique way. For example, Bob Hope used a line during some of his military jaunts that said, "I came over here in a jeep. You all know what a jeep is—that's a New York taxicab that's been drafted." He was relating the jeep to a New York cab.

In another famous line Bob Hope used when he was emceeing the Oscars, he said, "Welcome to the Academy Awards, or as we call it at my house, Passover." The idea here was that he related the awards ceremony to his being "passed over."

The more references you can accumulate, the more joke ideas you'll have running through your mind and the easier it will be to generate usable lines. You'll not only be able to write more lines, but also better lines.

Sub-divide. Now try to break your main topic down into several sub-topics. The purpose of this is to help focus on a smaller segment of your premise. For some reason it's easier to write five jokes on five different sub-topics than it is to write twenty-five jokes on the main premise.

For the example shown above, I divided my main topic, the Schuylkill Expressway, into these sub-topics:

a) What's it like driving on the Schuylkill Expressway?

b) What does the word mean?

c) How scary it is to drive on the Expressway.

d) How scary it is for others to drive with you on the Expressway.

e) You pray a lot while driving on the Expressway.

Now begin writing lines on each of your sub-topics. I recommend at least four or five lines on each sub-topic. Why so many if your column is only going to be eight to twelve gags long? Over-writing gives you the luxury of editing out the weaker gags and only including your best. It makes for cleverer comedy.

Many comedy writers quit too soon—on both their topics and their jokes. Once they generate a gag, they're satisfied with it. One of my colleagues once called me a pioneer in comedy. I asked what that meant. He said, "You're an early settler." It wasn't a compliment. Settling for the first idea you get keeps you from digging out the really creative lines. Often with a little more time and effort a joke can be improved considerably or even replaced with a much stronger line.

If you find one sub-topic particularly fertile, continue writing gags on that. There's nothing wrong with writing a good series of one-liners on just one or two sub-topics.

Now select your strongest one-liners and arrange them in a logical sequence. I used to cut the individual lines into small strips of paper and physically rearrange them on the desktop. When I had them properly sequenced, I would staple them together and then retype them in that order. The conveniences built into today's word processing software makes this step much easier.

Rewrite. Now that you've determined the order of your lines, you can see where rewrites are required. Since your gags were written independently, you may find some repetitive wording that needs rewriting. You may spot places where transitions are required. Sometimes, just reading through this final sequence will inspire new jokes that seem to "fit right in."

Now your monologue column should be sharp, creative, polished, and ready for submission and sale.

Chapter Twelve

Random Gags

Like the monologue form, this type of humorous article is also made up of one-liners that are on a specific topic. In this case, though, the gags are free-standing, rather than arranged in a logical, conversational flow.

In one sense these are easier to write than the monologue form, since the jokes aren't required to be in any logical sequence. In another sense, though, they could be considered more difficult writing because the gags do have to stand on their own merit. They can't draw any comedic support from the surrounding lines.

Since the flow and the sequence of your lines are not important in this type of article, you don't have to edit these pieces as meticulously as you do the monologue style. Nevertheless, for marketing purposes you should be aware of the sequence of the lines you submit. Try to arrange them in such a way that you maximize their effect, even if only for the editor. Even if your initial lines make a strong impact, you don't want the humor to wane as the editor reads on. Once you get that interest, you want to maintain it.

There are no set rules for arranging random lines in an effective order. As a humorist, you use you intuition and "seat-of-the-pants" feel for comedy to keep your writing interesting.

As I mentioned, the now defunct *McCall's* magazine used pieces like this as the last page of their monthly, in a column called "To Leave You Laughing..." I sold many such pieces to *McCall's* and as an example of this style of humor writing, I'll list here both the material that I submitted, in the form that I submitted it, and the final selections that the editors published.

The following submission was for a September issue. The premise was that September is "Back to School" month.

The School Bus is Here, Hooray, Hooray

Real tears are shed on the day you send your children back to school—by the school bus driver.

It's "back to school" day, or as they call it in the teacher's lounge, "round one."

The house will seem empty on that first day the youngsters go back to school. In fact, it will be empty; you'll be out celebrating.

Thank heaven for "back to school" day. Parenting would be impossible if it weren't for those five blessed words: "No, tomorrow's a school day."

Compared to the pure joy you feel when sending the children back to school, Mother's Day becomes purely symbolic.

How come when the children go back to school each year they're just about one year older, but you've aged five?

Remember, you haven't lost a son when you send him back to school; you've gained a car-pool assignment.

The first day of school is tough on the children. They only have about six hours to figure out why they can't stand their new teacher.

It's hard to believe, but the youngster who goes off to school this morning with not a care in the world, will be three days behind in her homework by the time she gets home.

All summer you've been after the children to pick up their toys. Now you'll be after them to pick up their grades.

It's a sad day for parents when the children return to school. They know it's less than 30 days till the bills come in for their "back to school" clothes.

The youngsters don't really mind going back to school. They know Mom was just about at her breaking point anyway.

Science has yet to figure out which is louder on "back to school" day: the happy chatter of the children inside the school bus, or the sigh of relief from the mothers outside.

Mothers are eager to send their offspring back to school. If the school bus got a flat tire, they'd fix it. If it got four flat tires, they'd carry it.

One problem with school children having three months off each year is that nine months is not enough time for parents to recuperate.

You know it was time for the kids to go back to school when you return from seeing them off and find the family pets are all wearing party hats.

There are many good things about school and education. After three months of having the kids at home, the best thing about it is that it's not held in your house.

The children look so sparkling bright and clean on that first day of school. They all look like they're "for sale."

So the children are finally back to school. Just think, in 8 to 10 days you may have their rooms cleaned up.

This should give you an idea how tough mothers have it during vacation: all of us have had to write a "What I Did During the Summer" essay. None of us ever wrote about picking up our toys.

The worst part of getting the kids out of bed and ready for school is that you usually have to get out of bed yourself to do it.

There are twenty-one gags in this submission for a piece that normally would include no more than seven to ten lines. As we noted earlier, overwriting affords you the luxury of editing out the weaker lines and keeping the stronger ones. By submitting more than required, you're giving the editor that same convenience.

The finished page featured seven of my lines along with my byline. It also printed four cartoons having to do with "back to school" day.

Below is the article as printed, with the gags in the order in which they appeared on the page. See if you feel there is a synergistic effect caused by which gags were selected and by the order they appear.

To leave you laughing . . .

Relief—At Last

By Gene Perret

How come when the children go back to school each year they're just about one year older, but you've aged five?

It's hard to believe, but the youngster who goes off to school this morning with not a care in the world, will be three days behind in her homework by the time she gets home.

All summer you've been after the children to pick up their toys. Now you'll be after them to pick up their grades.

There are many good things about school and education. After three months of having the kids at home, the best thing about it is that it's not held in your house.

When Junior goes back to school, you won't be losing a son; you'll be gaining a car-pool assignment.

The first day of school is tough on the children. They only have about six hours to figure out why they can't stand their new teacher.

Raising kids would be impossible if it weren't for those five blessed words: "no, tomorrow's a school day."

Tips on writing

For this type of article, follow the suggestions in the previous chapter on the monologue form, except that you can omit steps 5 and 6 since they don't apply here. In their place, as we said earlier, use your comedy instincts in arranging your lines in the sequence that you feel maximizes their effect.

One caution, though. You do have the luxury of submitting all of your gags and letting the editor select the best for publication. You don't really have to edit out any in order to fit a logical sequence. In this instance, even gags that are contradictory can be included. You certainly wouldn't do that in the monologue form. But, do some editing anyway. Overwriting is a plus here because it is a convenience for the editor. However, pure quantity won't help you make a sale. Twenty good lines is a good selling point. Forty lines, though, with only twenty good ones among them may not be a good marketing ploy. Leaving too many inferior lines in your submission could be counter-productive. Including weak gags in your submission could work against your sale even if you do have enough usable gags for the column. They could possibly create a negative impression on the editor. Only include gags that you feel are representative of your writing skill.

Don't showcase your "duds."

Chapter Thirteen

Laundry Lists

The Laundry List is a series of one-liners in random form, also. However, in this style, there is one set-up line followed by a "laundry list" of items that play off of that set-up. The classic example is one created by comedian Jeff Foxworthy—"You know you're a red-neck when..." Foxworthy uses this device in his stage act, but he's also authored several books based on the same premise. He and his writers have come up with hundreds of punch lines to that one straight line.

Jeff Foxworthy's work is also a powerful example of how much material can be created when enough references are accumulated.

This following laundry list example was submitted to *McCall's* for a January issue. My premise, and the title of the piece was "Silly New Year's Resolutions That Just Aren't Worth Making." Here again, I'll show the column as I submitted it to the magazine and then the final article as it was published.

Silly New Year's Resolutions
That Just Aren't Worth Making

Don't resolve to...

...clean out your spouse's sock drawer. One year is not enough time.

...teach your children to speak without using slang. You may be better off not knowing what they're saying.

...to get better organized. It annoys you if you fail, and your friends and loved ones if you succeed.

...teach the family pet to be better behaved around company. Dogs make resolutions of their own, you know.

...clean out the freezer. What you recognize, you'll want to stay frozen; what you don't recognize could be dangerous if allowed to thaw.

...be more patient and understanding with your children. It just forces them to work harder to find new ways to annoy you.

...keep the house straightened up and spotless all the time. After all, your family has a right to know where their shoes are.

...diet and exercise regularly. Cellulite needs a place to live, too.

...attend more Little League games. The kids like it better when you don't.

...write those letters you've been putting off. Most of those people have moved by now anyway.

...learn more about your husband's work. You may find out his boss has been right and he's been wrong all these years.

...give up sweets, fried foods, and rich, creamy sauces. Remember, the spirit is willing, but the flesh has it surrounded.

...take up jogging. The payment on the shoes will last longer than your resolution.

...have a quiet hour each day with the children. The words "quiet" and "children" cannot coexist in the same hour nor the same sentence.

...pay all your bills on time. If you succeed, it just reaffirms your debtors' contention that they haven't been charging you enough.

...do more things with your children that they like to do. They like to do those things because they don't hurt when they get up the next morning like you will.

...live within your budget. Why should you be better than your government?

...be better at anything. It'll just make you worse at something else.

...take that vacation this year that you want, deserve, and need. One year is not enough time.

Happy new year anyway.

The finished page featured seven of the submitted lines along with my byline. It also printed four cartoons having to do with New Year's Day.

Below is the article as printed, with the gags in the order in which they appeared on the page:

To leave you laughing . . .

New Year's Resolutions You Shouldn't Bother Making

By Gene Perret

Don't Resolve to…

...teach your children to speak without using slang. You may be better off not knowing what they're saying.

...keep the house straightened up and spotless all the time. After all, your family has a right to know where their shoes are.

...clean out the freezer. What you recognize, you'll want to stay frozen; what you don't recognize could be dangerous if thawed.

...be more patient and understanding with your children. It just forces them to work harder to find new ways to annoy you.

...teach the family pet to be better behaved around company. Dogs make resolutions, too, you know.

...live within your budget. Why should you be better than your government?

...give up sweets, fried foods, and rich, creamy sauces. Remember, the spirit is willing, but the flesh has it surrounded.

In the above example, the set up is always the same—"Don't Resolve To …"—but the items in the laundry list are really stand alone lines. Notice that they include a set-up line, followed immediately by the punch line. Another form of laundry lists, truer to the format, is one in which you have a standard set up, and the items in the list following it are the punch lines to that constant straight line.

Following is an example of that form of laundry list:

It's Time to Diet and Exercise When...

...you try to do a few pushups and discover that certain body parts refuse to leave the floor.

...your children look through your wedding album and want to know who Daddy's first wife was.

...you get winded just saying the words "six-kilometer run."

...you come to the conclusion that if God really wanted you to touch your toes each morning, He would have put them somewhere around your knees.

...you analyze your body honestly and decide what you should develop first is your sense of humor.

...you step on a talking scale and it says, "Come back when you're alone."

...to you, "Itsy-Bitsy Teenie-Weenie Yellow Polka Dot Bikini" and "The Impossible Dream" become the same song.

...you accept the fact that you can fool some of the people all of the time and all of the people some of the time, but not while you're wearing a bathing suit.

Tips on writing the laundry lists form

The suggestions for writing this type of humorous article are exactly the same as in the last chapter—Random Gags.

Chapter Fourteen

Essay

Someone asked George Burns once what the difference was between a comedian and a humorist. Burns said, "If I get big laughs, I'm a comedian. If I get small laughs, I'm a humorist." Then he added, "If I get no laughs, I'm a singer."

Some readers might be tempted to ask about now, "What's the difference between a gag writer and a humor writer?" All of the humor article forms we've discussed so far—monologues, random gags, and laundry lists—have all dealt primarily with jokes.

This chapter, though, is the breaking off point. This is where we separate the gagsters from the humorists. Now you can flex your literary muscles. You can manipulate your metaphors and sneak in your similes. You can have your poetic prose dance around the page. This is your chance to become a literary figure…not merely a jokester.

The essay form is where you get to editorialize about whatever you feel like editorializing about. This is your chance to be eloquent. You can now say what you think as lyrically as you like.

In this form you decide on your major topic and then pose your incisive observations about that topic. No lowly gags are required, unless you decide to include a few. One-liners are not *de rigueur*. In fact, unless the one-liners are used judiciously and appropriately, they can seem out of place in the essay form.

One caveat, though: Referring back to George Burns's quote at the beginning of this chapter, you'll notice that the legendary comic said, "If I get big laughs, I'm a comedian. If I get small laughs, I'm a humorist." Notice in both cases, though, he got laughs. Without laughs he became a singer.

In writing humorous essays, your primary objective is to be humorous. You can write as powerfully as Hemingway, Fitzgerald, King; but if you don't amuse, you're not a humor writer. Unless you entertain your readers and cajole a chuckle or two, you're not writing humor. You may be writing informed op-ed pieces, or investigative journalism, or remarkably learned treatises. You're not writing humor.

One time I was reading several of my jokes to Bob Hope for a show he would be doing later in the day. After I read one, he stared at me and said, "That's not very funny." I defended my writing, though. I said, "That's true, Bob, but it has impact. If you deliver that line in front of tonight's audience, you'll get applause." I put a big emphasis on the word 'applause.' Bob Hope just kept staring at me for a beat or two, then said, "How long have you been writing philosophy?"

Humor writers should not write philosophy, either.

This doesn't mean that you can't convey a strong message in your piece. It also doesn't imply that you must write only on lightweight topics. For a good example of a serious subject treated with wonderful humor, read a few chapters of the book *Eats, Shoots & Leaves* by Lynne Truss. This is a book dealing with punctuation, not often considered fodder for funny writing. And the author doesn't trivialize her subject. She takes punctuation quite seriously.

Yet the book is amusing. It entertained enough people to make the best-seller charts in England and in the U.S.

You can write about serious subjects and you can make profound observations, but you must do it with humor. Of course, you are welcome to write about serious subjects and make profound observations without humor, but then, again, you're not being a humorous writer.

The essay is a list of your questions or opinions about a particular topic. In a sense, your observations are really the "jokes" in this form. They may not be stated in a one-liner style, but there should be a kernel of a gag in there somewhere. That kernel may be expressed in a well-written paragraph, or maybe two or three paragraphs, but somewhere there should be something resembling a punch line.

A television producer once advised our writing staff that in order to have an effective joke, we had to tell the audience when to laugh. At the time I thought it was a simplistic statement. In fact, I didn't like this producer very much so frankly I thought it was a dumb statement. However, I later found it quite beneficial.

Just to illustrate, consider that some comedy performers think they are so hilarious that they could get laughs by reading the phone book. That's kind of clever bit of hyperbole, but one comic believed it. He came on stage at a comedy club and read the phone book...for over half an hour.

Is that funny? Yes, it's funny to recount, but it wasn't much fun being in the club that night. Why? Because there's no specific point where it becomes funny. There's no place where the audience knows when to laugh.

So even in writing humorous essays, you must include some hint to the readers that this is an amusing piece of writing.

I don't write many humorous essays. Most of my writing now is in the forms that we'll be discussing later in the book. However, this following piece about everyone in the Arizona desert regions defending the climate by insisting, "It's a dry heat," is an example of the essay form of humor writing.

The Great Arizona Cliche

It happens to every mid-summer visitor to Arizona. With some it's as soon as they step off the plane or drive across the state line. Others may wait a day or two. Only the strong willed can resist for a week or more. Sooner or later each one of them will say, "Yes, but it's a dry heat."

Even people who don't want to say it, say it.

"How are you doing?" a passerby greets you.

"Not bad," you reply in a neighborly way.

"Hot enough for you?" the stranger asks. Now that's a strange question.

Why are folks asking you if it's hot enough? Were you appointed "Temperature General of the United States?" Do they ask other people if it's hot enough for them? Suppose you say it is hot enough for you and another says it's not hot enough for him. A debate, even a fight, could start. Strange question. But you answer it.

If you're in Arizona you answer it with, "Yes, but it's a dry heat."

You didn't want to answer it like that. You promised your-self you would never respond with such a trite phrase, but you did. Why? The answer is simple: you're in Arizona and it's the law.

Arizona wants to promote her dry heat. It may someday be the motto on license plates. "The Dry Heat State," or "Soggy Summers—never had 'em; never will," or "Arizona—Where You Simmer but You Never Soak."

But what does the cliche, "It's a dry heat," mean?

It's meant to be conciliatory. Folks are saying, "Look, I know you're suffering in these unreasonably high temperatures—the permanent has drooped out of your hair, your walking shoes have melted—but look on the bright side. It's a dry heat."

How is that supposed to cheer anyone up? It's like being in Beverly Hills and having a car back into you, snapping your knee cap into three pieces, and someone consoles you by saying, "Yeah, but it was a Mercedes Benz."

It's like being attacked by a rabid dog, and having someone comfort you with, "That's a nasty series of bites you have there, but it was a short-haired dog."

> "I suppose dry heat would be preferable to being captured by a roving band of cannibals, set into a pot of water with assorted herbs and vegetables, and boiled until tender."

What consolation is it? One implication is that dry heat is preferred, but to what? I suppose dry heat would be preferable to being captured by a roving band of cannibals, set into a pot of water with assorted herbs and vegetables, and boiled until tender. Now that's a wet heat. And it is uncomfortable.

Basically, the cliche is meaningless. Yet Arizonans hear it so often, they begin to take pride in it. "Yes, we have dry heat here and we're doggone proud of it. If we could find a way to symbolize it, we'd include on the state flag."

Some Arizonans even believe it. Mark Twain once said that everybody talks about the weather but no one ever does anything about it. Well, here in Arizona we do. We dry our heat before we serve it to you. There's rare, medium rare, medium well. We can even give it to you well done, if you like, but we don't guarantee it.

Someone also said that two things are certain in this life—death and taxes. In Arizona in summertime, two other things are certain—heat and people saying, "Yes, but it's a dry heat."

I wonder, though, if the opposite is true. Do tourists flock to the northernmost reaches of Alaska in the middle of winter, and proclaim to the natives, "Yes, but it's a wet cold"?

Tips on writing the essay form

Begin this composition like you would any other writing project. Do your research, make notes, assemble your observations and finalize your opinions, arrange all of this in a logical progression, make your outline—either on paper or in your head—and begin your writing.

As an example, the above essay article might have been outlined like this:

1) People in Arizona say, "It's a dry heat."

2) Why does anyone ask, "Is it hot enough for you?"

3) Why do Arizonans respond with, "It's a dry heat"?

4) It's probably considered good PR for the state.

5) How can that "dry heat" phrase cheer anyone up?

6) Basically, the phrase is meaningless, yet Arizonans take great pride in it.

7) If this phrase were true, would the opposite be valid, also?

What makes the humorous essay different from other forms of essay writing is…well…it's the humor. There must be something in it that prompts the readers to smile, chuckle, guffaw, or choke on their own laughter. In addition to organizing your material, you must search out the fun in your topic.

As we noted, in previous forms that this book has discussed, the humor was generally in the form of short jokes or one-liners. In this form, the humor can be more drawn out. It can be in a longer form. It just has to be there.

You begin finding this type of humor the same way you mined gags in the earlier pieces—you find references, relationships, something in the topic that lends itself to humor.

> *"What makes the humorous essay different from other forms of essay writing is...well...it's the humor. There must be something in it that prompts the readers to smile, chuckle, guffaw, or choke on their own laughter."*

Here again, it's a good idea to let the idea marinate. Do your preparatory work and then set it aside for a brief period. This might be a couple of hours or it might be a day or two. If the idea is set in your mind, you'll continue to generate thoughts on it somewhere in your subconscious even though you're not actively working on the project.

When you're ready to begin finalizing the piece, focus on those ideas that are ironic, contradictory, or intriguing about your topic. Begin to find those relationships that can generate some funny writing. You can do this by investigating your topic thoroughly and seeing if any ironic relationships pop out at you. If they do, note them. Then you can dig further into the subject by making factual statements about the topic and then trying to add a punch line. Again, of course, the punch line in this form doesn't have to be a one-liner or a quick joke. It can be paragraphs long if you like. Then you might begin to ask questions about your topic. Sometimes you'll find that the answers to these questions can provide fodder for your humor.

As an illustration, let's suppose that we're going to write an article about self-help books. One idea that pops out at me immediately is that if they were truly *self-help* then you wouldn't need a book to guide you. Maybe they should be called *self-help books for those who are incapable of helping themselves.*

As an offshoot of this idea, it seems that it might be hard to find a good self-help book. You go to the information clerk in the bookstore and say, "I'd like to find a good self-help book." Wouldn't she say, "Find it yourself?"

Among the factual statements might be that most of these books cite examples of people who used the principles in the book and accumulated great wealth and success. Sure, they gather riches while all you've got is this cheap paperback. That might lead one to write:

> **In this particular book they listed a guy who tried this formula. He started with $57 in his pocket and now he has a mansion in Florida, a huge yacht, a Rolls Royce and a several million dollar bank account. Sure, he got millions, a mansion, a yacht, a Rolls; and all I got was this crummy self-help book. If I was this guy I would have gone from $57 to $40.05 because the stupid book costs $16.95.**

Another fact might be that these authors tell you you can do anything you want, yet all they can do is write self-help books. That might lead to an observation like this:

> **This man tells me it's my own fear holding me back. I can walk across a plank on the floor with no problem, but put that board ten stories in the air suspended between two buildings, and all of a sudden I'm afraid to venture the walk. Then I'm expected to go to a book signing, buy his volume, and have him autograph it for me. No. Instead of him sitting behind the desk in the store, I want him to go up to the tenth floor, walk across a thin plank to the building next door, come down the elevator, sit calmly behind the desk. *Then* I'll buy his book and have him sign it.**

Then you might ask questions about this topic. Are the premises in this book valid? Are the titles misleading? Is the author qualified to write this type of book?

The answers to some of the questions you pose can uncover some funny observations:

These books often tell you that you can get anything you want. Well, suppose you want to get this book for free. They don't tell you until the last chapter, that's called "shoplifting."

I really bought into the self-help craze and I bought a book because I wanted to own a nice new car. I faithfully followed all the suggestions. I made lists, I meditated, I offered encouragement to myself. And while I was spending all this time trying to convince myself that I deserved a luxurious new car, they repossessed my Toyota.

Some of these books have contradictory titles. I have a hard time figuring out this one: *Self-Esteem for Dummies.*

I tried everything this author suggested and nothing worked for me. I got no richer; I got no more successful. So, I did the only thing I could do. I wrote a self-help book of my own. I called it *Secrets of Success for Those People Who Can't Do Anything Else.*

Once you have noted your observations, you might consider wording that will intensify the humor. Obviously, a good humor writer writes things in a humorous way. Often it's the way you say something that gets the chuckle from the reader. For instance, earlier we had an observation about going into a book store and asking the clerk for help in finding a self-help book. She said, "Find it yourself."

Maybe there's a better way of expressing that same idea. For instance:

> **I have an awful lot of trouble finding a good self-help book. I'm just too ashamed to go to the information clerk in a bookstore and say, "I'm looking for a good book on self-help. Can you help me?"**

Is that better than the original? It's a personal choice. However, there might be another way of wording it that could be more humorous than both of these. Spend a little bit of time reworking your phrasing, not just for the literary value, but to intensify the humor.

Once you assemble all these thoughts into logical form and create your outline, you're ready to write a great humorous essay.

Chapter Fifteen

Parody

Consider this sketchy plot outline for a humorous article:

A gentleman is lunching with several friends. He tells them he is getting married again. As a Christmas present he has given his lady an engagement ring. They try to talk him out of it, pointing out that with three ex-wives he's not been very lucky in the matrimonial arena. He's not dissuaded, although they have planted some doubts in his resolve.

That night during his sleep he has a bizarre experience. He's visited by the ghost of Johnny Carson, the oft-married former late-night TV host. Carson is weighted down with heavy chains.

"I'm Johnny Carson," the apparition says.

The man says, "I know who you are. But what are those heavy chains you bear?"

Carson says, "Alimony payments."

Carson warns the man that during this night he will entertain three visitors—the ghosts of past wives one, two, and three.

The apparitions do visit him separately, and take him to visit uncomfortable scenes from each of his previous marriages.

By the end of the evening, the man realizes what a poor husband he has made in the past and that he will probably be just as incompetent in the upcoming marriage. In the morning, he is going to call his girlfriend to try to cancel the nuptial plans.

She answers the phone, but before he can talk, she tells him that she had the strangest dreams last night. She was visited by the ghosts of his ex-wives.

> **Even though they visited him the night before, he pro-**
> **tests, "That's impossible. All my ex-wives are living."**
> **She says, "Sure, now that they're not married to**
> **you any longer."**
> **She wants him to take the ring back. He agrees.**
> **In unison they say, "Merry Christmas, one and all."**

Does that sound familiar? Sure it does. It's supposed to sound familiar. That's a take-off of Dickens's famous *Christmas Carol*.

That's parody.

The dictionary says that parody is a literary or musical composition imitating the characteristic style of some other work or of a writer or composer, but treating a serious subject in a nonsensical manner in an attempt at humor or ridicule.

The example above is a replication of the plot of Dickens's work. However, parody can also parallel the style of certain writers. Periodically, there are contests in which writers try to duplicate the concise Hemingway style. I've often seen writers try to get some humor from writing modern day pieces with a Shakespearean flair…for example, a western gunfight written by the Bard.

> **"I've halted my steed in this village for the sole purpose**
> **of delivering your soul, knave known as Bart of Black, back**
> **to your creator. Being a fair and just man, unlike thyself, I**
> **give thee leave to draweth thine own firepiece before I essay**
> **the unholstering of mine own. Maketh thy move, oh, villain**
> **with paunch of yellow and liver not unlike the beautiful**
> **flower that groweth in the fields beyond."**

Well, you see now why the dictionary added those words, "…in an *attempt* at humor or ridicule.

I don't have a personal parody to list as an example. I don't write much in that style now for two reasons. First, I'm not very good at it. Second, I've had my fill of parody writing from when I was working for television and performers.

In Bob Hope's concert act, he would always do a song or two and we writers would have to come up with a different parody at each performance based on whatever was the hot topic in the news or where he was appearing. Hope would do over two hundred appearances a year. That's a lot of parody writing.

In fact, he used to do a song parody that didn't change with the current headlines. It was based on his travels around the country. He would do special material about different places that he had visited. There were about twelve segments to this song.

Hope was never quite satisfied with it and the writers worked constantly on changing one segment or another. Finally we got it to where it was almost perfect.

Bob Hope called and told me that all the parts were working well except for one. We writers worked on that one segment week after week and month after month but could never satisfy Bob.

One night Hope called and pleaded with me to have the staff get a solid line for that one section. He said, "The rest of the song is so powerful that it makes this section look very weak."

Anxious to get rid of this project, I called the other writers and persuaded them to develop some great special material so that we could make this last section as powerful as the rest and get this writing albatross from around our necks.

They came through spectacularly. I sent all the new material to Bob Hope and after his next performance, he called and said, "That new section works great. The guys really came through." I was pleased and relieved until he added, "But now it makes the other eleven spots look weak. Have the guys work on those."

Tips on writing parody

Pick a subject that's recognizable. In the example that was used to open this chapter, you probably recognized after one or two sentences that this was based on Charles Dickens's *Christmas Carol*. The other example was based on Shakespearean prose. Now whether I duplicated William's melodic prose or not, is up for argument, but the style was apparent. It would be worthless to do a take-off of Kenneth

Grahame's *The Wind in the Willows* or to try to do a gunfighter scene in the style of William Barnes. No one would know the story or the style.

Referring back to my television writing days, we did plenty of movie parodies on both *The Carol Burnett Show* and the Bob Hope specials. Carol preferred to do comedy take-offs on the classic films. Hope would do sketches about the current blockbusters. The Burnett sketches, though, had to be based on old films that were classics, otherwise the viewers would have no frame of reference. You can't do a parody on *any* movie that was made in the 1940s—only those that are well-known and fondly remembered.

Hope wanted to kid the current hits. He wanted the films that were getting lots of press and that people were talking about. You couldn't kid a flop. No one would know what you were talking about because not enough people had seen the film or even heard about it. No one would get the connection. With the boffo films, though, even the folks who hadn't yet seen the film would know enough about it, because of all the press coverage and the word of mouth, to appreciate the comedy references.

Night club comic impressionists typically do impersonations of Marlon Brando, Jack Nicholson, Jimmy Cagney, Jimmy Stewart—voices that people know. Very rarely will you see one do an impression of Millard Fillmore.

Likewise in your writing, parody something that is known and recognizable. That doesn't mean it has to be on a literary work. You can parody the latest hit television show or film. You can do a take-off of a well-known personality in your work. For instance, you might do an article that has some fun with say Andy Rooney as your family doctor. "It's a funny thing about measles, isn't it?..." You can parody anything that is parody-able.

Which brings us to the next tip.

Parody only what is parody-able. O.K., that's not a word, but we'll see in a later chapter that it's O.K. for humorists to manufacture new words. Parody-able denotes a topic that can be parodied. Some topics are not good parody material because they're almost a parody of themselves. It would not be a good idea to parody a Dave Barry column, for example. Parody is a tongue-in-cheek look at your subject and Barry writes with a tongue-in-cheek style. There's room for only so many tongues in a given cheek. Besides, chances are that Barry's column would be funnier than the take-off.

Generally, you look for a subject that is serious, even pompous. Will Shakespeare's dialogue, to the modern ear, sounds stilted. Put his flowery phrasing into the mouth of a gun-fighter, a sports announcer, or a marine drill instructor, and you get funny results.

Earlier I mentioned the movie take-offs on the Burnett and Hope shows. They were always about serious films; rarely comedies. Comedy doesn't lend itself readily to parody.

Parody is a tool of ridicule. It's much easier to make fun of someone who is high-falutin', dignified, pompous.

> "Parody is a tool of ridicule. It's much easier to make fun of someone who is high-falutin', dignified, pompous."

Include recognizable elements in your parody. Sustain the references throughout your parody. For example, in the earlier selection that showed a gun-fighter speaking in Shakespearean dialect, notice that he called his adversary, "…villain with paunch of yellow and liver not unlike the beautiful flower that groweth in the fields beyond." That's Will's way of stating the common cowboy put-down, "You yellow-bellied, lily-livered coward." The article also transposed the common western moniker, "Black Bart," into the more Old English form, "Bart of Black."

Also in the *Christmas Carol* knock-off, Johnny Carson was loaded down with chains just as Marlowe was in the original. In the parody, though, they represented alimony payments.

A major feature of parody is that the readers recognize the connections and the references. Just as with the nightclub impressionist, the audience should recognize the voices. Including recognizable references throughout will keep your parody alive.

Chapter Sixteen

Sketch

I spent five glorious years on the writing staff of *The Carol Burnett Show*. It was a wonderful writing experience for many reasons.

The creativity was always fresh and new. Working on a weekly sitcom can get cloying. You always have the same characters and after a while, you begin to redo the situations and the premises. I recall watching a taping of one sitcom with the rest of the writing staff on a television monitor in the producer's office. After about five minutes one writer stormed out, saying, "I'm sick of this family." On a production like the Burnett show, the characters could change from week to week. The premises could vary, also. The writing was always fresh and intriguing for the writers.

There were few limitations on what one could write. On a sitcom, of course, the premises are limited by the family of characters. "Fraiser Crane wouldn't do that." "Will would never do that to Grace." In fact, I once suggested that the ideal show to work on would be *The Muppets*. Those characters couldn't object to the writing. You simply send them out once a month to be dry cleaned and that was that. Then, fittingly enough, I worked on a show featuring the Muppets. Sure enough, one of the folks who operated the hand puppets said, "Miss Piggy would never act like that." On the Burnett show, since we created the characters that we wanted for each sketch, they wouldn't have prejudices. They would say and do whatever the writers wanted them to say and do.

The cast on this show, too, were very appreciative of the writing. They would work very hard to make the words on paper work on screen. On some shows, the performers would work against the writers. It's a tremendous advantage for both the show and the writers to have the actors cooperating with the creative staff.

Another reason I enjoyed *The Carol Burnett Show* was because, with the staff, I collected three Emmys during the five years I worked on the show.

However, what does all of this have to do with writing humorous magazine articles? There is a form of writing comedic pieces for publication that is very similar to writing sketches for variety shows. All of the advantages I mentioned above pertain, too. You can vary your topics and your characters from piece to piece so your writing is always interesting and fresh. You can pretty much write about whatever you want. And finally, your characters can never object to your writing because they exist only on paper. The people you put into your "sketches" will always be cooperative.

We'll discuss three different forms of the sketch format:

1) **The episodic form**
2) **The progressive form**
3) **The bit**

The episodic form: This format consists of the same formula repeated several times. Basically, the story is static. It doesn't move forward from point A to point B to point C and so on. It simply keeps repeating point A. In essence, nothing much happens except that we generate laughs along the way.

Our hero in the episodic piece has a goal. He tries one idea to achieve that goal. That idea fails. He tries another. That fails, too. He comes up with yet another idea which proves just as futile. This sequence continues until there is some sort of resolution, some fitting ending.

Notice, though, that nothing is actually changing as the piece progresses. The main character always has the same problem. The plot doesn't move forward. Often, the plot points are interchangeable and not locked into a chronological sequence. The piece is a series of episodes that are amusing, to be sure, but as far as the story goes, are repetitive.

The Roadrunner cartoons you see in the theatres are a good example of this type of story line. Wile E. Coyote wants to destroy the Roadrunner. That's his goal. He devises some sort of booby trap loaded with cartoon dynamite. The dynamite doesn't go off. When Coyote goes to see what the problem was, the dynamite blows him sky high and leaves him burnt like a piece of toast.

In the next scene, though, we see a revitalized Wile E. Coyote trying another scheme. He paints a fake tunnel into a mountain hoping that the Roadrunner will knock himself senseless trying to run through it. Of course, the Roadrunner does run through it just as if it were a real tunnel. When the confused Coyote looks into the tunnel, a train roars through it and runs him down.

In the next scene, Coyote is planning yet another attack...then another...and so on until the end of the cartoon.

That's basically the episodic form.

Following is an example of a humorous article written in that form.

Easy Openers

I'm a man. I open pickle jars. I was born to open pickle jars. We men open pickle jars better than any other gender on earth. This is not another chauvinistic boast of male superiority; it's a humble confession that, aside from pickle jars, there are so many things that confound us. Take what happened today for example...

My wife left early this morning and I had to fix my own breakfast. I had to open a new box of cereal. The engineering on cereal boxes is ingenious and practical. They provide a tiny tab that once the package is opened will fit into a tiny slot, thus encouraging you to close the box after each use and keep the contents fresh and crisp for a longer time. The instructions on the carton were simple enough—place finger under tab and lift. What these instructions don't tell you is that the flaps of this carton are glued together with the same adhesive that holds airplane wings on.

When I lifted flap A, I horribly mauled flap B, totally destroying the little slot that the tab is supposed to be reinserted into after each use. With flap A came 78 percent of flap B, 32 percent of the back of the box, and the first three steps of the marshmallow-cereal cookie recipe printed on the side panel. And I still hadn't gotten to the cereal.

The honey coated flakes mixed with raisins and nut slices are protected by a bag of some sort of indestructible paper that is welded shut and then the edges are run over by three or four Sherman tanks in succession.

Most of the houses in our neighborhood have little stickers on each window and a large placard planted in the lawn that warns: this house protected by armed response. Those houses would be easier to break into than this bag of cereal.

So I abandoned breakfast and decided to have brunch—crackers and cheese.

Conveniently, the package of cheese had a little red line of plastic running around the top edge. Again, brilliant engineering. The red plastic was embedded under the clear plastic wrapping. All I had to do was pull that red strip, as the printing on the package suggested, and I'd make a clean cut and be able to get at the individually wrapped slices of cheese easily.

But nowhere could I find any part of this little red string that was outside the clear plastic wrapping. I scraped at it with my fingernail, picked at it with a knife, poked at it with a fork. That little red line was under the outer wrapping and it was determined to stay under there. The only way to grab an edge of that red plastic was to be inside with the cheese.

I opted for crackers and crackers instead. The box of crackers was brilliantly designed to be easily opened, too. I was instructed to press my thumb against the red dot printed on the package and then run my thumb back and forth along the carton. This would snap open a lid that could be easily opened and securely closed with each use.

I pushed the red dot and felt something give, then I ran my thumb back and forth and it opened...not the box—a paper cut on the tip of my thumb that bled freely. I panicked too much to know whether the box of crackers ever opened or not. The bleeding had to be stopped, so I ran into the bathroom to get an adhesive bandage.

Thank goodness, the box was already opened. But the individual bandage was not. Some clever team of package designers again provided an easy way of getting to the contents. I had to tear off a little piece of the plastic wrapping. This would expose a tiny red string. I was to pull the string down the side of the wrapper, fold open the flaps, and there would be the handy bandage for my wound. The problem was the tiny red string came off with the little piece of plastic that I tore from the top. It was now totally useless.

I fiddled and fussed with the bandage, but couldn't get it out of its wrapper. Maybe when I was healthy I could have done it, but with a sore thumb, it was almost impossible. It didn't matter anyway. The bleeding had stopped.

However, the headache, which I didn't have when I woke up but I had now, was throbbing. The aspirins were in a child-proof bottle. I was to push down on the lid while at the same time turning it in a counter-clockwise direction. I did. I heard a loud click. Each time I turned it I heard a loud click, but I never heard the bottle say, "Hey, I'm opened now. You can just lift the lid and take out a few aspirins to ease your pain." I never heard that.

I never had breakfast that morning, either. I left for work a defeated man.

The saddest part of this tale is that a when I got home that night, I noticed in the refrigerator there was a jar of pickles that had been opened. It was unopened when I left. My wife must have opened it while I was gone.

This piece does have a chronological flow to it, but it's of secondary importance. The main thrust is repetitive—there is something to be opened and the hero of the tale can't get it opened.

The progressive form: In this style, the story moves forward. It has a chronological progression. Each moment in the tale presents its own unique complications.

As in the episodic form, the hero has a goal. He tries plan A, which may or may not work. In either case, though, it leads to point B. This new plot point creates problems for the hero. He tries to solve them, which leads to point C. The story continues this way until the story is resolved.

In the episodic form the plot points are practically independent. You can move them around or delete entire episodes without destroying the flow of the tale. In the example of the Roadrunner cartoons, the fake tunnel can come before or after the dynamite. It makes no difference.

In the progressive form, though, each element leads to the next. Each part of the story is dependent on what went before it. They're intertwined and can't be rearranged or removed without extensive rewriting.

The following article is an example of the progressive form of humorous article.

Dining Out and Decisions

Dining out at one time was a relaxing experience. Someone else would cook for you, serve you, and clean up after you. All you had to do was chew, swallow, and pay for the food. No longer, though. Lately dining out has become a stressful event. Take today, for example. I went out for a nice relaxing dinner and here's what happened…

"Good evening," the maitre d' said. "Table for four?"

I said, "Yes, thank you."

He said, "Smoking or non-smoking?"

I said, "Non-smoking."

He said, "Would you prefer to dine indoors or out this evening?"

I said, "Oh, gee, I don't know. I guess indoors would be good."

"Very well, sir," he said. "Would you like to be seated in the main dining room, the enclosed patio, or our lovely solarium?"

I said, "Oh…uh…let me see…uh…"

He said, "I can give you a table with a lovely view in our lovely solarium."

"I think the solarium would be lovely," I said.

We all followed him into the solarium.

He said, "Now, would you prefer a view overlooking the

golf course, the sunset on the lake, or the majestic mountains to the west?"

"Whatever you recommend," I said. Let him make a decision for a change.

He sat us by a window facing either the golf course, the lake, or the mountains. I couldn't tell which since it was dark outside.

The waiter came over. He said, "Good evening, my name is Paul and I'll be your waiter. May I take your order or would you like a few more minutes?"

I said, "You can take our order."

He began with me.

I said, "I'm just a meat and potatoes kind of guy so I'll have the filet mignon and a baked potato."

He said, "Soup or salad?"

I said, "Salad."

He said, "We have a mixed green salad, hearts of palm, or a very fine endive salad with baby shrimp."

I said, "Just a mixed green salad, OK?"

He said, "Whatever you say, sir. Dressing?"

I didn't want to make another decision. I said, "Whatever you've got will be fine."

He said, "We have creamy Italian, blue cheese, vinaigrette, thousand island, honey dijon, ranch..."

I said, "Just bring me one of those."

He said, "Which one, sir?"

I said, "Any one, O.K.? Surprise me."

He said, "The creamy Italian is our house specialty. Would that be all right, sir?"

I said, "Yeah." I was curt. I was done with civility.

He said, "And your baked potato..."

I knew what was coming and I didn't want any more questions. I told him, "I just want the baked potato dry, you understand? I don't want nothing on it."

He said, "No sour cream?"

I said, "No."

He said, "No chives?"

I said, "No." I said it louder.

He said, "No butter?"

I said, "Don't you understand English? I don't want nothing on it. Nothing. Just bring me a baked potato and a piece of steak."

He said, "Would you prefer the six, eight, or twelve-ounce steak, sir?"

I said, "Whatever."

He said, "Would you like to have that rare, medium rare, medium, medium well, well-done, or if you prefer, we can butterfly that for you, sir?"

I said, "You know something, Paully Boy, you're really starting to get on my nerves. You're really starting to get me steamed."

He said, "Which brings up the vegetables, sir? Would you like steamed broccoli, creamed corn, sauteed zucchini, diced carrots and peas, asparagus tips..."

I threw my napkin to the floor. "That does it," I said. I put my face right up to his arrogant kisser and said, "How'd you like to settle this outside?"

He said, "That's fine with me, sir. Would you prefer the parking lot, the side alley, the back entrance, or the street in front of the restaurant?"

I said, "I prefer right here," and I sucker punched him.

He ducked. I missed him totally but he countered with a left hook right under my eye. It was the first time all night he didn't offer me a selection.

I collapsed back into my chair in a state of semi-consciousness. I could hear everything going on about me, but my body just didn't care to get involved. I heard the "oohs" and "ahs" of the people nearby. It sounded like someone in authority rushed over and berated our waiter. How could he do such a thing to a customer? Didn't he realize this could cause a lawsuit?

I felt my tie being loosened and my collar being unbuttoned, hands slapping my face to awaken me. When I regained my senses, I saw the very concerned maitre d' right in front of my nose. He apologized, offered to buy me a drink, to call the paramedics—whatever I wanted.

I said, "No, no. I'll be all right. Just bring me glass of water."

"Yes sir," he said. "Right away. "Would you prefer imported mineral water, bottled water, sparkling water, flavored water, or simply club soda with a wedge of lime?"

Yes, at one time dining out was a relaxing experience. But not today.

Notice that in this piece, you can't have the waiter come to the table before the maitre d' seats you in the restaurant. There is a definite and unchangeable continuity to the piece.

The bit: This style doesn't require a story or a plot. It simply needs an idea. It needs something that will produce and sustain humor. Usually it's just one idea.

Allow me to refer back to television for some examples of bits. Jack Benny would often do a bit on his radio and television shows which you might remember. It was strictly one idea, but it produced big laughs. I'll paraphrase some of it here to jog your memory. Mel Blanc in this routine was a man who spoke only Spanish, with a pronounced accent. It went something like this:

Benny: Are you from around here?
Blanc: Si.
Benny: Do you work here?
Blanc: Si.
Benny: So you have a name?
Blanc: Si.
Benny: What's your name?
Blanc: Sy.
Benny: Sy?
Blanc: Si.

Benny: Do you have a sister?

Blanc: Si.

Benny: Does your sister have a name?

Blanc: Si.

Benny: What's your sister's name?

Blanc: Sue.

Benny: Sue?

Blanc: Si.

...and so on...

There's another good example from TV which you may have seen since it's been featured on many of the "Best of Carson" shows and tapes. It was a bit with Jack Webb of *Dragnet* fame.

In this one, Carson and Webb talked in the clipped dialogue that was a trademark of the *Dragnet* TV series. However, it was an endless series of alliterations. Practically every word they said began with the letter "C" or "K." It was a story about "Clem from Cleveland and the Copper Clapper Caper. Clem, the copper clapper keeper, was also a kleptomaniac." It went on and on and was hilarious.

It may be hard to duplicate this form as purely in the humorous article format, but it pays to be aware of it. Sometimes it can be coupled with the episodic or progressive styles to produce funny results.

Following is an article that I consider an appropriate example of "the bit."

I Have A Mind Like A Steel Whatchamacallit

Many factors can destroy an otherwise satisfying film—bad direction, bad writing, bad acting, bad memory. That's right, bad memory.

My wife and I were enjoying a well-directed, well-written, well-acted movie on television this evening when my wife commented on one of the young performers. She said, "I don't know who that actor is, but he's very good."

I said, "Yes he is very good. You know who he reminds me of?"

She said, "Who?"

I said, "A young…uh…whatshisname."

She said, "A young who?"

I said, "Oh, you know."

She said, "No, I don't know."

I said, "Oh, he's very famous. Everybody knows his name."

My wife said, "Except you and me."

I said, "I know it, but I can't think of it. Oh, this is gonna bother me. It begins with an 'R.'"

She said, "Burt Reynolds."

I said, "No…"

She said, "Robert Redford."

I said, "No…"

She said, "Rin-Tin-Tin."

I said, "You're not helping."

She said, "It doesn't really matter anyway what his name is."

I said, "It matters to me. I won't be able to enjoy this movie until I think of it."

She said, "Then I guess I won't, either."

I said, "This is going to bother me the whole evening. Let's see…Roman…Ryman…Regal…"

"Ronald Reagan," my wife shouted.

I said, "No, I would remember Ronald Reagan." I was getting frustrated.

Now my wife decided to try to be more helpful. She said, "What movie was he in?"

I said, "That one we saw a couple of years ago."

She said, "And the name of it was…"

I said, "I forget."

She said, "What was it about?"

I said, "I forget that, too. But anyway, this actor was in it."

She said, "The one whose name starts with 'R.'"

I said, "Right. Reed…Rod…Rumpole…Oh, I know. He was in this movie… ."

She said, "The one you don't know the name of and you can't remember what it was about."

I said, "Yes…that's the one. He was in that movie with that actress."

She said, "Which actress?"

I said, "That actress I used to like."

She said, "Which actress you used to like?"

I said, "Oh, you know."

She said, "No, I don't know."

I said, "She was married to…uh…that guy."

She said, "Which guy?"

I said, "The big guy. The guy who got in a fight once with whatshisname."

She said, "The other guy?"

I said, "Yeah, the other guy. They got in a fight."

She said, "Over the actress you used to like?"

I said, "No, this was a whole different thing. In fact, they did a thing on it the other night on that television show."

She said, "Which television show?"

I said, "You know…the one I can't stand."

She said, "Which one you can't stand?"

I said, "The one with the guy and the girl as the hosts."

She said, "You know who we're beginning to sound like?"

I said, "Abbott and Costello."

My wife said, "How come you can remember Abbott and Costello but you can't remember whatshisname?"

I said, "Don't get mad at me. I can't help it if I can't remember names."

She said, "You can't remember anything."

From then on we watched the movie in silence. Well, not exactly in silence; we just didn't talk to each other. I kept mumbling names that started with "R." "Ringo…Rango…Rumble…Rimble."

Then it hit me.

"Alan Ladd," I shouted.

She said, "Alan Ladd?"

I said, "Yeah. That's the guy this actor reminds me of—a young Alan Ladd. Doesn't he?"

She said, "No."

I said, "Well, that's who he reminds me of, Alan Ladd."

We watched in silence a little longer.

My wife said, "How do you get an 'R' in Alan Ladd?"

I said, "I think I'll go make some popcorn."

The basic idea here, of course, is that the hero can't recall names or titles. The entire piece is based on that one premise.

Tips on writing

A humorous article in the sketch format is pretty much the same type of piece that you would write for a variety show. It features characters and it tells a story about them. A story must have a beginning, a middle, and an end. Typically a story has a goal, some obstacles to achieving that goal, and then a resolution.

Referring back to television writing again, young writers often object when veterans explain that in sketches and in sitcoms, the premise is paramount. They feel that the jokes are most important, since we are dealing in comedy.

Yes, gags are important. The teleplay should get laughs. However, it's the story that keeps the viewer intrigued, tuned in. The writer should focus on making the story interesting and believable and then the jokes will flow from that story line. If the gags are the main focus, the writer usually produces just a string of jokes tied together tenuously. That makes for weak story telling.

The same applies to writing humorous articles in the sketch format. The premise is most important. What are you trying to say in this witty piece? That's the first step in writing a humorous article in the sketch format—settle on and define your premise. It's a good idea to express your premise in a sentence or two. For example, the premises of the pieces I used to illustrate would be:

1) Things that are supposed to be designed to be easy to open

are not always so easy to open—at least not for the fall guy in this article.

2) When you go out to dine, you're bombarded with endless questions and choices.

3) Sometimes a name you know well escapes you—along with almost everything else.

Then, of course, keep your premise before you as you write the article.

Next, as with most of the other forms of humorous articles, let the idea marinate. Give it an hour or two, or even a day or two to settle into your mind. Decide, too, whether you'll write your article in the first person or the third person. You've probably noticed that I like to star in my own articles, and I do prefer the sketch form. I find it easier to write in the first person and I think it's funnier and safer if I'm the fall guy in my humorous articles. You may prefer to write in the third person. Either way is fine.

Then begin to accumulate a few jokes or funny pieces that you can incorporate into your article. Start building up some ammunition for your writing.

After you've accumulated enough material, you assemble these segments into some logical sequence. In the episodic form and the bit form, the segments need not be locked into a chronological flow; nevertheless, you will want to put them in an order that maximizes their comedic effect.

In the progressive form, you'll want to generate a time line or sequence of plot points. What happens first? What does that lead to? What would most likely happen after that? Continue on until you resolve the story.

Now you're ready to write an hilarious article.

Chapter Seventeen

Fillers and Short Ancedotes

Most people associate these kinds of pieces with *Reader's Digest*. The fillers are the short, one-liner type of humor that are found, either alone or in a grouping of several, filling out space at the bottom of a page or the end of an article. For example, here's one of mine that *Reader's Digest* published after it first appeared in *McCall's*:

> **It's time to diet and exercise when you accept the fact that you can fool some of the people all of the time and all of the people some of the time—but not when you're wearing a bathing suit.**

The short anecdote is the type of gag that *Reader's Digest* publishes in their humor departments, such as "Life in These United States," "Humor in Uniform," "Campus Comedy" and the like. These are usually items of about three hundred words or less that can be either true or apocryphal, depending on which department they're published in. Here's an example:

> **My fellow workers used to kid me about my "unhip" clothes. One day I showed up for work wearing a new pair of shoes that I thought were sporty and hip. My colleagues didn't agree. They kidded me about my silly looking shoes, too. I tried to get them to let up by telling a fib: "You guys can kid if you want, but these shoes were given to me by my dear uncle on his deathbed." One fellow looked again at my shoes and said, "What did he die of—embarrassment?"**

These pieces offer a high return for a small amount of work. *Reader's Digest* pays about $300 for a short anecdote for one of the departments, and about $100 for a short one-line filler.

Reader's Digest is not the only periodical that buys this type of humor. The first gag I ever sold was to a Sunday supplement magazine. I still remember the submission. It read:

There's no such thing as a Sunday Driver anymore. They're all Friday Drivers still looking for a parking space.

Arizona Highways encourages readers to send in gags and short anecdotes for their monthly "Humor" page. At present they're paying between $50 and $75 per item.

Many publications will publish short pieces of humor. It's just a matter of searching through the magazine racks to find them or doing some research with a good writing market list.

Tips on writing

Shakespeare admonished that "brevity is the soul of wit." The Bard was partially right. These pieces should be short. One reason is because humor has a cost/reward ratio. That is that readers and audiences expect a certain payout from their punch line consistent with the amount of time they invest. The longer your gag setup runs, the bigger the laugh has to be. If you spend a long time developing your setup and the joke is weak, you get a groaner. The readers are disappointed. Therefore, it pays to keep it short. "Brevity is the soul of wit," as Will S. reminds us.

However, brevity is not the be all and end all of humor. A very concise joke is Henny Youngman's classic, "Take my wife...please." It's four words long and got howls when it was still a young gag. Today, the payoff is less because more people know of it, but it's considered a classic one-liner. It's almost the perfect joke.

However, if we make it even shorter, or briefer if you want to be a purist in following Shakespeare's advice; we can say, "Take my wife." There. That cuts a whole word out of the joke. It's briefer, but it's no longer funny. It now has no punch.

So brevity is the soul of wit, provided we have enough information in the telling, to let us know where and what the humor is.

Fillers and anecdote writing should be efficient. It should deliver enough information to the readers so they know what the punch line is. In other words, the piece must be long enough to get the comedy across, but not so long that it weakens the comedic effect.

For instance, in my earlier example about being kidded about my "not too cool" shoes, I mentioned that it was my fellow workers who razzed me. However, it's not important that I mention where we worked or what we did. The readers didn't have to know what shift we were on. They didn't have to know whether we were gathered around the water cooler or not. Many of these facts might have been included, but they would have lengthened the setup and weakened the effect of the punch line.

Be frugal with your facts and your verbiage in writing short humor. Give enough information to get the laugh, but not so much that you destroy the laugh.

With this type of short humor writing, you need a punch line. You need a laugh at the end of the telling. Here's a tale that provides a nice laugh:

> **At an awards banquet, Bob Hope was to present an award to a blind golfer. When the golfer reached the podium, though, Bob Hope couldn't resist kidding him. He said, "Blind golfer, huh? I'd like to play you some time."**
>
> **The golfer replied, "I'd love to play a round of golf with you, Mr. Hope."**
>
> **Hope said, "I don't think you understand. I only play for money."**
>
> **The honoree said, "I don't mind a little side bet. It makes the game more interesting."**
>
> **Now Hope was a little scared. He said, "But you're a blind golfer. What kind of a handicap would you want me to give you?"**
>
> **The gentleman said, "Mr. Hope, I'll play you even up."**
>
> **Hope was delighted. He said, "Name the time."**
>
> **The blind man said, "Midnight."**

Notice that the punch is on the final word of the story—"midnight." That one word gets the reaction. That's a punch line.

Any story that needs a handle to influence the readers is weak. For example, you tell your story, but then have to add "Everyone cracked up with laughter." That's not a good anecdote. Just tell your story and let the readers "crack up with laughter."

If your anecdote absolutely needs that ending phrase, it's not a good anecdote. The tale should be able to stand on its own. It should have a punch line that needs neither explanation nor reinforcement.

There's one other suggestion that might help with these short pieces. We touched on it earlier in this book. The advice is to *let the other guy have the laugh*. Readers might think it too boastful if you always have the clever comeback, the quick retort. They would rather that you, the author, be the fall guy.

You don't want readers to resent you; you want them to be entertained by your story telling. You make it easier for them if you are the brunt of your own jokes rather than the brilliantly clever "quipmaster."

Once I played tennis with a good friend and I passed him with a dazzling shot right along the line. He looked at me and said, "Just remember, I hold a grudge for a long time." Meaning, of course, that he would remember that shot and get even with me.

I responded, "The way you play tennis, I imagine you would have to."

It was a nice adlib, if I must say so myself. I wrote that story up and sold it to a magazine as a short anecdote.

Except in the piece I wrote, my pal hit the passing shot and delivered the punch line to me.

Readers seem to prefer that.

There are a few drawbacks to writing these pieces. First, you do have a lot of competition. The editor who used to select the humor for *Reader's Digest* once lectured at one of my comedy writing seminars. She quoted the number of submissions that they received each month and it was staggering. This is understandable because almost everyone has an uncle who told a funny story or a child who said something cute and precocious. Whenever they tell that story, people say, "You should write that up and send it to *Reader's Digest.*" Many of them do.

However, there's an upside to that, too. This same editor pleaded with the aspiring comedy writers at the seminar to send material to the *Digest*. The obvious question, which one of the students asked, was, "If you get so many submissions, why are you asking us to send in more?"

She responded, "If you know humor and have a good sense of comedy timing, which all of you at this class do, you have an excellent chance of standing out among so many dilettantes."

Again, the quality will show. This editor wasn't necessarily asking for more submissions. She was asking for more *good* submissions.

> ● "**B**e frugal with your facts and your verbiage in writing short humor. Give enough information to get the laugh, but not so much that you destroy the laugh."

Another drawback that you should be aware of is that most magazines will not return fillers and short anecdotes. This *Digest* editor pointed out that since the number of submissions was astronomical, even if you include the self-addressed stamped envelope, it was prohibitive to hire people to just put all of these submissions back into envelopes and mail them back.

You may send a few submissions in and not hear from the publishers for a year or even two. Then you get a letter saying that they're considering using such and such a joke in an upcoming issue.

It's not the best way for a free-lancer to work, but it is the way it is with this type of writing. However, since they take such little time to type out and submit, it's probably worth it.

The *Digest* has made it even easier to submit. Now you can send jokes in for consideration via e-mail. According to the information in the front of the magazine, you simply go to RD.com and click on "submit a joke." However, it still will probably take quite a few months to hear any type of response...if at all.

Sometimes, though, you might get an editor who is favorable to your submissions. They all want good comedy, and general readership submissions are not always that dependable. If an editor knows he has a writer he can count on, you may have an almost guaranteed sale with each of your submissions. Then you probably won't have to wait that year or two for a return. You may not know which gags are selected, but you'll be fairly certain that some of them will be.

In sending in short anecdotes or filler lines, type each submission on a separate sheet of paper and be sure that your name and return address are on each sheet. It's tempting to type ten or twelve on one page and send them in, but it's not to your benefit.

As I mentioned, the editors may hold certain submissions for over a year. Also, certain selections may be sent around to other editors for consideration before being published. It's simply easier for the staff if the jokes are all separate. They don't have any cutting to do, or separating of any kind. Each submission is up for sale, so keep them one to a page. You will have a better chance of making a sale.

PART III

General Tips on Writing Humor

Chapter Eighteen

Which Type of Article Should You Write?

There are four considerations in deciding which type of article you should write:

1) Which type do you want to write?

2) Which type do you write best?

3) Which type do the buyers want?

4) Which type will sell?

Let's analyze each consideration individually.

1) Which type do you want to write? Way back in chapter one we noted that writing humor was fun. That premise still functions. So write whichever format you most enjoy.

Are you a story teller? Write the sketch format or the short anecdotes. Do you relish offering your opinion? Write the essay format. Maybe you have always delighted in reading the classics. Then write parodies of them.

Me? I loved jokes. Will Rogers and Bob Hope were my heroes. I relished listening to all of the current comics and devoured their material. I would read all the short humorous pieces in *Reader's Digest*, even clipping some out and saving them for future reference. I scanned the gossip columnists for the latest *bon mots* from the celebrities. I loved one-liners. So I wrote them.

That's one benefit of writing what you enjoy—you have a built-in interest in the genre. Because of your fascination, you've been getting a liberal education subliminally. For years, you've probably been studying that format without even realizing it. You know a lot more than you think you know about that style of writing.

Also, you probably have a natural talent for this particular writing style. You most likely have an intuitive feel for it. Combine this with the knowledge you've assimilated and you will find you have a fairly advanced writing technique for that particular format.

Since you've been reading or listening to this stuff voraciously, you surely have an awareness of the markets. You knew where to look to read it; you know where to look to sell it.

You'll certainly write more and persevere longer if you're writing a technique that you enjoy. Writing what you like is seldom a chore.

These are all compelling reasons to write whichever type of article you most enjoy.

2) You're a professional writer, though. That means you expect to make money from what you write. As we mentioned earlier, the way to successful writing—successful *anything*, for that matter—is to be good at what you do and to continue to get better at it. Therefore, it makes sense to write something that you're already pretty good at.

How do you know which format you write best? Well, let me begin with a story that has nothing to do with writing—or does it?

I grew up not eating crab cakes. I didn't like them, so I didn't eat them. I was kind of like President Bush the first who declared that since he was president of the United States he didn't have to eat broccoli. I held no high office, but still declared that I had the right not to eat crab cakes.

Then my wife and I went on a golfing outing with several friends. We stayed at a nice resort where all of the golf was prepaid and so were the meals. One night, the chef served small crab cakes as appetizers. Being as frugal as I am, and since the appetizers were already paid for, I ate one.

It was delicious.

Now, my wife and I go out perhaps once a month on a Friday night so that I can enjoy a plate of crab cakes at a favorite seafood restaurant.

Somewhere along the way, I decided that I didn't like crabmeat. I had never even tasted it, but I knew I didn't like it.

The moral of this tale? Try the crab cakes.

Give each of these formats a try. You may discover that one you thought would be difficult for you comes rather easily. You could be surprised to find that some writing you thought you wouldn't enjoy, you do.

I recall at one comedy writing seminar, we handed out an assignment to the writing teams. They were to come up with titles and authors for some of the "Shortest Books Ever Written." To give you some examples: "Johnny Carson Jokes I Haven't Laughed At," by Ed McMahon; "My Adventures in Pole Vaulting," by Roseanne Barr. Well, you get the idea.

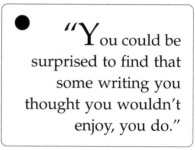

● "You could be surprised to find that some writing you thought you wouldn't enjoy, you do."

At this particular session we had several guests in the back of the room. They weren't enrolled in the comedy writing seminar, but were onlookers. They were friends of some of the attendees, but they were folks who readily admitted, "I couldn't write a funny joke if my life depended on it."

As the writing teams were working diligently on their assignment, they were distracted by loud laughter from these spectators. The back-of-the-roomers were writing their own jokes and passing them around. Obviously, they were getting big laughs.

We collected a few of their gags and read them to the class. They were hilarious. People who "couldn't write a joke if my life depended on it" were not only writing some boffo gags, but also delighting in the process.

They surprised themselves (and us). You might surprise yourself, too.

Try writing all of the styles. If I had tried the crab cakes earlier, I would have known that I relished them. If you attempt a few of these writing styles, you might find that you have a natural talent for one or more of them that you never suspected you had.

Experimenting with the different formats is good writing training. It forces you to be innovative and to think as a writer in ways that you don't normally. It can only be a plus.

3) What type of article is the market buying? This is only common sense for a professional writer. If you want to sell something, it pays to know what the buyers are buying. That was one benefit of having an agent in the television and film arena. A good agent had a close relationship with producers. He or she would know what the networks, the production companies, the film studios, and even the stars were looking for. NBC wants a sitcom that such and such a young comic can star in. Universal wants a film about aliens. So-and-so has been off the air now for two years. Her managers are looking for a good variety show format she can host.

These are all definite wants and needs. Come up with an idea for any one of them and you'll get a meeting with the executives. As a writer, you're not spinning your wheels; you're working on a project with built-in sales potential.

The same logic applies to selling humor to magazines. If the magazine has a definite need, why not fill it? I mentioned earlier that *McCall's* used to end their periodical with a page called "To Leave You Laughing..." Each month they needed a page of gags on an appropriate subject, and they paid very well. I wrote a couple for them and then the editors would contact me and tell me which topics they wanted to pursue in upcoming issues. If that's what they wanted, that's what I would write.

Greeting card companies buy random gags from free-lancers. To break in, you write joke cards and submit them. If they like your writing, they may include you in their stable of free-lancers. They will let certain preferred writers know which subjects they want material on and perhaps which type of material they're most likely to buy. This is valuable inside information that any free-lancer would be glad to have. It also would be insane for a writer not to take advantage of it.

So try to know what the markets are after and then write that type of material.

4) Write the style that will sell. Wait a minute, isn't that the same as the consideration we just considered? Isn't that writing what the markets are seeking? Not necessarily.

Throughout my career I've seen many times when conventional wisdom was thwarted by good writers with good ideas. There was a time when "the people in the know" said that the networks would not buy any shows about bars or drinking. Then *Cheers* became a major hit. "Variety shows are dead," the pundits proclaimed. *Saturday Night Live* has been running continuously since that pronouncement. "The one thing that our magazine cannot publish is humor," one editor told me. "Our readers simply won't accept it." Within the year, that same periodical published three or four humorous pieces, all of which finished near the top of the reader surveys.

Yes, if you know certain buyers have a need and you can write to it, write to it. You can't pass up sales potential like that. However, at the same time, don't reject a good idea that you feel you can write just because rumor, tradition, or even a pronouncement from some executive declares that it won't sell.

Consider this example: Hollywood big-wigs and entertainment journalists forecast the end of Mel Gibson's career if he insisted on producing "The Passion of the Christ." The doom and gloomers, who were supposedly in the know, predicted that he would not only lose face in the film business, but that he would bankrupt himself since he invested his own money to produce the film.

Gibson produced the film. It was a smash. He made a fortune. All of those who said it would be a monumental box office disaster are now scrambling to get scripts in a similar vein so they can cash in on its coattails.

The moral of this tale is that if you have a project that you believe in and feel you can write, write it. It may be more difficult to sell, but if it sells, it could be a trailblazer.

A good writer is not condemned to write only what has been written before. Mark Twain wrote in a rebel style. He wrote novels using a southern dialect. It was a new approach to writing novels. Yet he became the premier American writer. Literary people scoffed at it, but the public loved it. His novels about Tom Sawyer and Huck Finn made Twain a fortune and probably the most popular humorist of his time ... arguably of all time.

When I was beginning to write humor, not many papers published a front page column of jokes on current and local topics. However, I enjoyed writing that sort of material. When I proposed it to some suburban newspapers, a few bought it. The columns were well received by the readers.

Good writers should know what will sell. Often, they know it better than the people who are buying. It may take some fabulous writing, and a bit of guile and salesmanship, but if you believe in yourself and your talent, it will be worth the effort.

Actually, though, these four considerations run together. When you consider one, you almost automatically consider one or more of the others, or at least a part of the others. You write the type of article you enjoy, but you probably enjoy the type of article that you write best. You want to write articles that the buyers want because you want to sell, but you also feel that whatever article you write well should sell.

So which style you write is up to you. It's a personal choice. I think it's wise to try all of them. As we said, you might surprise yourself. Besides, working in different genres improves your writing skills regardless of the writing you specialize in.

I remember one gentleman I used to play tennis with. During warm-ups, players generally hit a few ground strokes back and forth, then they exchange a few volleys, and finally, they hit a couple of overhead smashes. When I offered this gentleman some overheads, he refused. He said, "No, I'm no good at hitting overheads so I never practice them."

Shouldn't it have been the other way around?—"I never practice overheads; therefore I'm no good at hitting them."

Trying new styles may not lead to a new career for you, but it will help to make you a more rounded, versatile writer.

If you write and submit articles in several formats, the marketplace may decide where your real potential lies. If you're selling regularly, there's your niche.

I like the quote of the great magazine humorist Robert Benchley. He said, "It took me fifteen years to discover that I had no talent for writing, but I couldn't give it up because by that time I was too famous."

Maybe the marketplace will make you famous, too.

Chapter Nineteen

How to Write Funny

Admittedly that's a presumptuous chapter heading. In fact, people often ask me, "Can you really teach someone to write funny?" The answer is a definite yes…and no. I usually respond by asking, "Can you teach someone to run faster?" "Can you teach someone to be stronger?" Probably not. Yet, most major league teams have a speed coach, a strength coach. They have coaches for a lot of attributes that you can't really learn. In fact, in basketball, they say you can't teach someone to be taller. Yet, they do have instructors who help the big guys use their height to advantage.

So, no, you can't teach someone to be funny. However, you can teach some tricks that will help someone who has a natural bent for humor to enhance those skills. I know that some of my professional colleagues, who have read my books on writing for entertainers, have told me that some of the suggestions helped them write more quickly and to improve the quality of what they wrote.

That's the meaning of that boastful chapter heading. We'll discuss some professional tips that might help you utilize the natural abilities you already have for writing humor.

1) "Funny" is basically an attitude. It's a whimsical, irreverent, tongue-in-cheek look at practically everything. Once I was at a party and a gentleman there had just learned that I was a humor writer. He didn't seem to care for that much. When someone else asked what I did, he answered before I could. "He's a professional wise ass," he said.

I didn't take kindly to that remark, but I also couldn't honestly deny it. It's a coarse way of summing up what humor writers do.

Develop that "wise ass" outlook, but try at the same time to find a more genteel name for it.

2) You've often heard the saying, "Humor is a serious business." Well, it is. At least, part of it is. Generating humor requires some investigative effort and some analytical work, too. You must discover relevant facts and dissect them. You must pull your premise apart to find out what makes it tick.

To become a good humorist, devote a goodly amount of time to the preparatory work. Your writing not only becomes more incisive, but you'll find that you'll give yourself more ammunition for creating humor.

Most writers who do prepare also claim that it helps them write faster, too. That means the checks arrive sooner.

3) To write solid humor that strikes home with your readers, you should keep informed. Learn not only to know as much as your audience does, but also to think like your readers.

Allow me to relate another boastful story:

> **Before I became a professional humor writer, I would entertain at company banquets, twenty-five-year parties, retirement parties, and the like. I had a good fan base at the company where I worked. I wasn't very high up the management ladder. In fact, that was one of the jokes I used on occasion—"I'm low man on the management totem pole. That means I have a lot of wooden heads above me."**
>
> **Yet, during one struggle between management and labor, the top brass invited me in to the strategy sessions. When I asked why, the chairman of the committee said, "You seem to know what the workers are thinking."**

Yes, I did know what the workers were thinking because that's what I had to talk about each time I spoke to them at a party. I accepted this as a compliment not so much to me, as to the power of writing humor.

Often a good chunk of comedy is just expressing what many people are thinking in a way that they never would have thought to express it. It's a clever, inventive way of saying what people are thinking. To do that, you must be aware of what your readers are thinking.

Most of this knowledge can be acquired intuitively or through observation. Some, though, you can only obtain through research. As I mentioned earlier, in doing my routines about fellow workers, I would set up meetings with friends of the guest of honor and ask what they kidded him about, what his hobbies were, what some of his shortcomings were, where he went to school, what sort of student he was. In short, I'd ask about anything that might help me to write "inside" material about the person being honored.

You'll enhance your humor writing skills if you get to know what's current and what's popular. The hipper you become, the hipper your humor will be.

Part of my job as a writer who traveled with Bob Hope on his military jaunts was to do research. While Hope was making personal appearances and doing press conferences, I was talking to the enlisted folks.

My job was to find out what they liked and disliked about this particular base. I'd want to know where the good eating places and the bad eating spots were. I'd try to find out what they did for fun in this particular spot and where they could go to get into trouble. I'd even probe to find out some of the shortcomings of the commanding officer.

I'd incorporate this information into the comedy routines and when Hope would deliver the monologues in front of the GIs, it would hit them right between the eyes. Some of them would wonder how Bob Hope knew so much about their base.

Your humor should produce the same effect on your readers.

4) Surprise is not only an element of humor, it's the essential element. Comedy is really a contest of wits. To illustrate, let's take a look at the shortest form of humor—the one-liner.

This gag form usually has two main parts—the setup and the punch line. A nightclub comic says to his audience, "My brother-in-law is not really lazy. He's just superstitious."

That's the setup. What happens now? The audience, because they're familiar with this form, know that a joke is coming. They immediately start to write their own punch line to that joke in their heads.

Then the comic, with perfect timing, delivers the punch line— "He refuses to work on any day that ends in a 'y'."

It gets a laugh. O.K., maybe not a big one in this case, but you see the point. Why does it get a laugh? Because it's a better joke than the people in the audience could come up with (or at least, it should be). The comic or the comic's writers had hours, days, or months to work on that gag. The audience had only a fraction of a second.

But mostly it gets a laugh because the audience has been tricked. "Wait a minute," they say. "That's not being *superstitious*; that is being *lazy*." They were had. They know they were had. They enjoy being had. That's what comedy is.

Suppose, for example, we change the gag a bit. Suppose the comedian says, "My brother-in-law is not lazy. He has agoraphobia. He's afraid to leave the house."

That won't get a laugh. There's no surprise. There's no trickery. Consequently, there's no humor. The listeners feel cheated rather than entertained.

Humor is purposely misdirecting your readers. You lead them along with one train of thought, then you change trains on them.

Will Rogers once wrote, "I belong to no organized political party. I'm a Democrat." That's beautiful misdirection. He told the readers he didn't belong to an organized party, but then he says he's a Democrat. That's a contradiction. Oh, wait a minute. He's saying that the Democrats are not an *organized* political party. Clever. Funny.

Notice, too, how the last word of that statement changes everything that went before it. Surprise!

To get that surprise element into one's humor, the writer must orchestrate the thinking of the readers. See how Will Rogers manipulated the mind of his readers. He led them to believe that he was denying being involved with any political group. That's not what he was saying, but it was definitely what he wanted anyone reading or listening to think he was saying.

In some of my lectures on humor, I would try an experiment with the attendees. I would read to them a small piece about a childhood friend of mine.

I was in the fourth grade and had this good buddy. This friend of mine was a mischievous soul who had an uncanny

ability to always get the both of us into trouble. However, my good pal's bubbly personality and powers of persuasion always seem to leave me holding the bag. My buddy would go scot-free and I'd be the culprit condemned to serve out the punishment...for the both of us.

Then I'd ask people in the classroom to give me a verbal description of my pal. Invariably, they'd paint a Huck Finn type of portrait. This person would be red-headed, freckle-faced. Then I'd tell them that *she* was nothing like that at all.

Notice that my description never said "he" or "she." It was peppered with "friend," "good buddy," "pal"—genderless words. But it was definitely designed to imply a male companion, and it did lean towards the Tom Sawyer-Huck Finn type of relationship.

I also used this device in writing a short piece poking fun at advice columnists. One excerpt read:

> **Dear Doctor Advice,**
> I am fifteen years old. I think that's old enough to wear lipstick, rouge, and eye shadow. But every time my mother finds it, she throws it out and punishes me. Please answer and tell me who is right.
> **Signed,**
> **Ralph**

"Signed, Ralph" is the surprise element.

5) You can often generate humor by coming at a particular topic from an oblique angle. What does that mean? Well, it's looking at your subject from a different perspective. Ask children to draw a picture of a person and they'll usually do it from the traditional view. They'll draw that person head on. Hardly ever will you get a view from overhead or even from the back.

That's the way most people approach a topic, too. They see the traditional perspective. Yet, a rear view might be funny. Take the way we all see the television news anchorman—seated behind a desk and wearing a shirt, tie and jacket. However, view that anchorman from the back and you may discover that he's not wearing any pants.

I was treated to a delightful example of viewing something from a different angle when I attended a movie a few years ago. The film opened dramatically with several soldiers in camouflage garb and make-up sneaking through a wooded area. The suspense grew as they advanced on a large house that was heavily guarded by the enemy. One by one they eliminated the sentinels. Suddenly they burst through the doorway with their automatic weapons at the ready. The people in the theatre were frozen in horror. Then someone in the audience yelled, "Trick or treat."

Obviously they weren't there to collect goodies for their Halloween bags, but some wag in the audience gave their actions that entirely new meaning. It got big laughs that the movie makers surely didn't intend.

That's looking at something from an oblique angle.

How can you use this in your humor writing? That's pretty much up to your own creativity in finding different ways of approaching your traditional subjects. As an example, I once did an article about a house being burglarized. Not really a very funny topic. However, I did it from the point of view of the family pet—the designated protector of the household.

At first the pet/watchdog is thrilled to finally get some action. At last, this critter has something to spark him into guard dog mode. "I'll bare my teeth and growl menacingly," the dog thinks to himself. "That'll scare away this nasty intruder. I'll show him who's boss even if he does have a gun...gun?" The canine now has second thoughts about his courage. What good are a set of exposed fangs against a 38-special?

The dog reasons that he probably shouldn't get involved. The thief probably wants silverware, jewelry, and maybe some electronic equipment. The dog doesn't care about any of this stuff. All the critter has of worth in the house are a couple of chew toys and a ratty old tennis ball. Why confront the burglar since he's not interested in carting away any of the dog's valuables.

Besides, the dog realizes that his owners haven't really treated him that well anyway. Over the years, they've treated him like... well...like a dog. They feed him scraps of food that they don't want to eat and a horrible, smelly dog food that is practically inedible. It was food fit for...well...fit only for a dog.

So, the dog befriends the intruder and points to where the valuables are stored.

It can be surprising how different a thing can be—and presumably, how funny it can be—when viewed from an oblique angle.

Chapter Twenty

How to Use Words Humorously

In Act II, Scene II of *Hamlet,* Lord Polonius comes upon Hamlet pacing and reading. He asks, "What do you read, my lord?" Hamlet's understated reply is, "Words, words, words." It's a very perceptive response.

Words are all that any of us can read. Words are the only tools we writers have available to us. Oh, maybe we can enhance them or clarify them with good punctuation or adding emphasis with italics or a bold font, but the words are paramount.

Writers convey ideas and we do that with the written word. All writers should treat them respectfully. Humor writers must treat them respectfully, but also playfully. We should have a little fun with them.

In this excerpt from an article I did about working with the *Society for the Encouragement and Preservation of Barbershop Quartet Singing in America,* I played with this group's acronymic name, helping the reader with the pronunciation.

> **Most of the members don't refer to the organization as the Society for the Encouragement and Preservation of Barbershop Quartet Singing in America. The reason is because most of these guys can't say that many words in a row without breaking into song.**
>
> **The Society for the Encouragement...and so on is more easily known as SPEBSQSA (prounounced S-P-E-B-S-Q-S-A).**

Below is an article based entirely on a playful use of the word, "Why," which is the name of a real town in Arizona.

Why?

I was reading through a listing of Arizona cities, towns, and villages the other day and it led to an interesting coversation. I said to my wife, "Did you know there was a place in Arizona called Why?"

My wife said, "What?"

I said, "Why."

She said, "Because I want to know what you just said."

I said, "I just said, 'Why.'"

She said, "I know you just said 'Why,' right after I said, 'What?' But I want to know what you said right before you said, 'Why.'"

(Sometimes when my wife and I sit alone in our den and there's nothing too interesting on television, we like to pretend we're Abbott and Costello.)

I said, "I said, 'Did you know there was a place called Why, Arizona?'"

She said, "Really? Why."

I said, "I have no idea why."

She said, "No, I wasn't asking why. I was just repeating the name of the town."

"Oh," I said.

She said, "That's a strange name for a town. I wonder why anyone would call their home 'Why?'"

Now I knew she was asking why so I repeated my previous answer, "I have no idea why."

She asked, "Is there a Who, What, Where or When, Arizona?"

I didn't notice any on the list I had been reading from so I said, "Probably not. What difference would that make anyway?"

My wife said, "Well, maybe they called the town Why because Who, What, Where, and When were already taken."

"That's a possibility," I admitted. It was a rather remote possibility, but I didn't bother mentioning that to my spouse.

She asked, "Is there a 'Whynot,' Arizona?"

I said, "It's not on this list, but what makes you think there would be one?"

She said, "Why not?"

"You have a point," I said. Again, it was a rather tenuous one, but there was no reason to debate it.

"There must be a Just Because, Arizona on that list," she said.

I checked. There wasn't. I told her so.

She said, "It's probably a suburb of Why and isn't listed on there."

"What makes you so positive there's a Just Because in Arizona?"

She said, "Because the two go hand in hand. Anytime you ask someone 'Why?' they'll usually say, 'Just because.'"

This entire conversation was beginning to give me a dull headache, so I said, "Well, anyway, I thought it was interesting that there was a town called 'Why' in Arizona."

My wife said, "And so you're just going to leave it at that?"

I said…"Yeah." The pause was because I was wondering what exactly she wanted me to do about it.

She told me. "You can't just raise a question like that and then leave it unanswered."

I said, "What question?"

She said, "Why?"

I said, "That's not a question. It's the name of a town in Arizona."

She said, "But why was it named 'Why'? That's the question and I won't rest until I know the answer and since you brought it up in the first place, I think you should resolve it."

So, I did some research. It was easier than trying to argue my way out of it. I checked the encyclopedia, some travel books, made a few phone calls to friends and I discovered why 'Why' was 'Why.'

I told my wife, "You should find this fascinating. The town of Why was formerly referred to as 'The Y'—as in the letter 'Y'—because it was at the junction of Arizona highways 85 and 86 just north of Organ Pipe Cactus National Monument. How about that?"

She said, "So it has nothing to do with the question, 'why?'"

"Absolutely nothing," I said.

She said, "Then why on earth did you bring it up?"

"Just because," I said.

Words can be complicated things. They're used to convey thought. They're used to conjure up an image in the reader's mind. However, at best, they can only be an approximation of that thought or that image.

Sometimes the words themselves are at fault. For instance, if something is described as "hard," is it rock-solid, or is it difficult? Maybe it is strong. Or perhaps it's unfeeling. "Hard" can denote any one of those.

Sometimes you'll hear a sports announcer comment that lane five is harder for this bowler than lane six. That doesn't mean that lane five is any more rigid than its next-door neighbor. It simply means that this particular bowler has more trouble getting the ball to behave the way he wants it to on this particular lane.

Sometimes, though, the confusion is caused by either the speaker or the listener. Anything that's spoken or written goes through at least four generations. What the speaker wants to say, what the speaker actually says, what the listener hears, and what the listener thinks he hears. In fact, we might add another generation—what the listener interprets from what he hears.

To show that the speaker may not say exactly what he intends to say, let me tell you a story about a field trip my high school took to Washington, D.C. All of us wore a special medallion that represented our school. It was almost part of our uniform.

As we toured one of the buildings, one of the guides noticed our medallions. He asked one of my classmates, "Do you fellows have to wear those?"

My buddy answered, "Oh no. They're strictly obligatory."

I'll use another example from my past to show that sometimes the listener doesn't hear exactly what has been said. I was a supervisor in a large factory. One of my clerks, an older woman, was a contact between our drafting office and the factory.

One day she came storming up to my desk, furious. She demanded a meeting with me and with her shop steward. I called the steward forward and heard her complaint.

It seems that one of the guys in the factory had insulted her with some sort of obscenity and she was not going to stand for it. She wanted him chastised and punished and she insisted that a directive be issued stating that something like this should never happen again.

It seemed odd because the factory workers generally got along well with this woman.

The shop steward and I went to the factory to investigate.

It turned out that one of the factory foremen noticed that this woman was in such a hurry that she was making notes on her paperwork with both hands.

He said, "Boy, I never knew you were *ambidextrous*."

That was what he meant to say and it was what he said. It was what she heard, too. But to her that word had some sort of foul meaning.

To see just how complicated some words can be let's select one word and search out the various meanings and sub-meanings of it. Let's use the word "house."

The obvious and probably primary meaning is that a house is a building, a home. However, it can also mean a bordello. ("She ran a house in the red light district.") It can signify attendance. ("Vaudeville performers would always peek through the curtain and count the house.") It can mean the auditorium or theatre. ("Is there a doctor in the house?") As a verb, it can mean "to contain." ("The museum houses a large collection of pre-historic pottery.")

You may uncover other uses for the simple word "house."

Try this yourself. Pick a few ordinary words and think how many different meanings they have. Go to a dictionary and you may be surprised to find that there are a few more that you hadn't thought of or perhaps never even heard of.

Often these secondary meanings can be used for humor.

For instance, there was a popular song a few years back called "Volare." The word "volare" is Italian for "fly." It's important to know that. Why? Well, just in case you're walking down a street in Italy sometime and one of the natives says to you, "Excuse me, sir, but your *volare* is open."

Words can change meanings over the years, too. *The Gay Caballeros* has a different meaning today than it did when Disney first made the movie.

All of these strange properties of words can be used for comedic purposes.

Word play

There are no real rules in using words humorously. The humor writer can play with and manipulate words in any way to create comedy, to generate laughs. If the way you use a word produces a chuckle in your article, it's a valid use of the word. It needn't be grammatical, nor does it have to be the accepted usage. You don't even have to spell it correctly.

Probably the greatest example of playing with words for comedic effect is the classic Abbott and Costello routine, "Who's on First." It has survived for years, and I challenge anyone to listen to it and not laugh. It's hilarious. It's a beautiful piece of comedy writing.

Yet, I had a writing partner—a *comedy* writing partner, no less—who insisted that this was a weak routine. Why? Because he felt it was totally implausible. There could be no baseball team with such names. No one would believe there was a team with such names. And since the names were vital to the comedy of the piece, it was therefore unacceptable as good humor writing.

But it got laughs. It established a long-running career for Bud Abbott and Lou Costello. It survived time and changing values. People still laugh at this routine today. It's hilarious.

Since it was written to get laughs, and since it got laughs—and continues to get laughs—it's a very acceptable, commendable, remarkable bit of humor writing.

Similarly, in your writing, you can use words incorrectly, injudiciously, incoherently, in-anything-you-want-ly. If they produce humor, you, the humor writer have used those words effectively.

Following are several devices for using words humorously. This is a homemade collection and some of the features may overlap. This list is by no means comprehensive and it can never be. No matter how many clever uses of words we categorize, some brilliant writer will come up with even a new comedic word device.

You are invited to use any of these tricks in your own humor writing, but also you're invited to create your own.

Tom Swifties: In an earlier book on comedy writing (*Comedy Writing Step by Step*, Samuel French) I included several comedy writing exercises. This was the most popular.

It may not be a device you can use frequently in writing humorous articles, but it is worth trying just to show you how you can use words cleverly and for comedic effect.

The "Tom Swifties" are one sentence jokes that use a double meaning for the -ly adverb. The -ly adverbs were used extensively in the Tom Swift series of children's books.

In the exercise I recommended that the reader write 101 "Tom Swifties." Why? Well, because it stretches you creatively. Anyone can come up with a few, but to knuckle down and create one more than a hundred means that you must give it some heavy concentration. You must FOCUS.

So here are just a few examples from that exercise. Maybe you can get to work and come up with 101 of your own.

Besides, it's fun.

"I forgot to mail the check to the electric company," the man said delightedly.

"All right, who stole my thermal underwear?" the hunter shouted coldly.
"It wasn't me," his hunting partner said warmly.

"I've just swallowed an entire window," the woman shouted painfully.

"Why, this chicken has no beak," the farmer pronounced impeccably.

"One should never try to force feed a lion," the trainer declared off-handedly.

Malapropisms: This is a form of word play that derives its name from a character in the eighteenth-century play, *The Rivals,* written by Richard Sheridan. I'm not sure whether Sheridan created this device or whether it was in use before and he simply made it popular by including it in his play. Mrs. Malaprop, a character in the theatrical production, always seemed to use the exact wrong word. For example:

"Why murder's the matter! Slaughter's the matter! Killing's the matter!—but he can tell you the perpendiculars."

The dictionary defines malapropism as a ridiculous use of words, especially through confusion caused by resemblance in sound. For the humor writer, it's best if those sounds are recognizably similar and if the confusion produces a double meaning.

"My husband and I have just bought a French prevential bed."

"Apparently I was too old for the infantry, but just right for the adultery."

Archie Bunker in the TV series, *All in the Family,* became sort of a modern day Mrs. Malaprop. He thought that Abraham Lincoln was assassinated by *Alexander Graham Booth.* He advised his daughter to be sure to take her *birth patrol pills.* When his wife, Edith, had woman problems, she went to see her *groinacologist.*

Norm Crosby built a comedy act largely around malapropisms. Crosby says, "Our house was built very close to a *blabbing brook.*" Also, "I love my wife. I use every chance I get to put her up on a *pedestrian.*"

Here are a few more delightful examples of malapropisms:

"My son got in a fight with the school bully and gave him a big Shriner. My son escaped completely unabashed."

"Her writing was completely ineligible."

"He has a record that is unparalyzed in political history."

Wrong use of words: Malapropisms are the use of the wrong word. This form is closely akin to it. It's using a correct word wrongly. For instance, when there was unrest in Chicago during one of the political conventions, then mayor Richard Daley, went on television to defend his police department's aggressive tactics. He said:

"The police are not here to create disorder; they are here to preserve disorder."

Here's another example:

"It was a terrible disaster. He decapitated his right arm."

And another:

I could not believe how lucky I got on this blind date. I couldn't believe I was sitting across from this gorgeous creature enjoying a first date with her. However, she did seem a bit withdrawn as we were enjoying our pre-dinner cocktails.
"You seem a bit pensive," I said.
"Oh no," she answered. "Just thinking."
I knew then I wouldn't have a second date with her.

Words used in wacky combinations: These are almost compound malapropisms. They're words or phrases that are chopped up and then scrambled together again. The results can be funny.

"This is not exactly rocket surgery."

How about this one paraphrasing a baseball play-by-play announcer:

"In trying to catch that fly ball he banged his head against the outfield wall. It's now rolling back towards the infield."

Here are a few jumbled words of wisdom:

Birds of a feather gather no moss.

A rolling stone flocks together.

A stitch in time is worth two in the bush.

Confusing phraseology: This one is pretty close to the preceding. It's saying something that makes no sense, but then again it might make sense, but then again it doesn't make sense...or does it? Maybe these examples define it more eloquently:

My mom had a way of dealing with my petulance. She'd say to me, "Don't you dare look at me in that tone of voice."

Hall of Fame catcher Yogi Berra is famous for his misuse of the English language and common sense, too. Here are a couple of his famous sayings that require a little bit of thinking to dislodge the logic:

"When you come to a fork in the road, take it."

"Nobody goes to that restaurant anymore. It's too crowded."

"I want all the players to line up in alphabetical order according to size."

Playfully changing the meaning of words or phrases: I first became aware of this writing trick when I was a youngster. I went with my sister to buy some pizza. Hanging on the wall of the pizzeria was a large sign that said, "Free pizza all day tomorrow." I noticed, though, that the sign was weathered, torn, and dirty. It obviously had been hanging there for sometime.

I asked the proprietor, "Is that sign true?" He said, "Absolutely."

I said, "Then how come it's been hanging there for so long?"

He said, "When you come back tomorrow for your free pizza, the sign will still be there."

I didn't get it yet, so I said, "So?"

He said, "It will still say 'Free pizza *tomorrow.*'"

Finally I was in on the joke. They were not only playing with my mind, but also with the word "tomorrow."

'Tomorrow' has a different meaning today than it will have tomorrow.

I recall once laughing at my cousin when she made a completely accurate, although ridiculous sounding, statement. I picked up an old newspaper and read aloud a statement about something that the paper said would be happening tomorrow.

She said, "Tomorrow. That's today because this is yesterday's paper."

Earlier we cited Henny Youngman's classic one-liner as an illustration of brevity, but it's also a good example of abruptly changing the meaning. In his act, he would say, "Now take my wife...please." It seems he's saying, "Let's use my wife as an example." But with that one word "please" he immediately changes the meaning. He's now pleading for someone to literally "take his wife."

Here are a few other examples:

Someone in our group asked the farmer, "I was wondering how long cows should be milked."

The farmer said, "The same as short ones."

A sports reporter once asked coach John McKay, after a disastrous loss, "What do you think of your team's execution?" McKay replied, "I'm in favor of it."

Misunderstanding words and phrases: The brilliant standup comedian Stephen Wright has a good example of this device. He says:

"I went to a restaurant and the menu said you could have any item on the menu at any time. I said, 'I'll have the French toast from the Renaissance period.'"

Here's another example:

I applied for a job once and the interviewer asked, "Does anyone in your family suffer from insanity?" I said, "No, they all rather seem to enjoy it."

Using real words in bizarre contexts: This is a device where you use the correct words correctly, but in strange situations. For example:

I had a dog once, but he had a nervous breakdown. It was my own fault. I named him "Stay." Training him was difficult. "Stay, come." "Stay, fetch." Obedience school finally drove him nuts.

And:

I had a dog once, but he died of exhaustion. I think it was my fault. I named him "Fetch." Every time I called his name, he'd run after a stick.

Using the idiosyncracies of certain words: Here the words seem to have an inconsistency built right into them. You can take advantage of those "flaws" for comedy.

The boss called me into his office for a friendly chat.
"You appear to be a disgruntled employee," he said.
"Oh no, sir," I objected. "I'm extremely gruntled."

As a youngster, I admit I did hang around with a bad crowd—a gang of uncouth youths. But I wasn't a bad kid. In fact, I was probably the only couth youth in the gang.

Daffy definitions: We've already seen that many words have several definitions, but there's always room for one more. Often the humor writer can define a word like it has never been defined before.

As an example, I once saw a joke button that read, "Vegetarian—that's an Indian word for 'lousy hunter.'"

Comic Ed Bluestone once said in his act,

"I'm a quadrasexual. That means I'll do anything with anybody for a quarter."

Use words creatively: Often a humor writer can get more out a word than that word ever thought it could give. It's like using words "above and beyond the call of duty."

I said to my wife, "I do plenty to help around the house."
My wife harrumphed. My wife is an expert harrumpher.
In fact, she finished second three times in the statewide harrumphing competitions.

Use words as understatements: Words can do more than is expected of them, but sometimes it's clever to let them do less, too. A good example of understated words is a cartoon that appeared in *The New Yorker* many years ago. It shows two fencers in the traditional white suits and fencing masks. One has lunged and struck, and the other's head is shown flying away from his body. The caption of the cartoon reads, "Touche."

Another example:

> I came into the room dressed for the party we were supposed to attend.
>
> "You're wearing that?" my wife asked.
>
> "Yes," I said, "That's why I put these clothes on."
>
> She said, "Well, you're not going out with me in that attire. Your tie is grotesque and it doesn't go with that suit. The suit is ill-fitting and it needs a pressing. Those shoes are not only out of style, but they look grungy. They need a shine. The whole ensemble is abominable and I refuse to be seen on the arm of someone dressed so abysmally."
>
> I said, "Quit beating around the bush. Do you like it or don't you?"

Make up new words: After one disastrous hole of golf, a friend of mine on the next tee hit the ball hard, straight, and tremendously long.

I said, "Nice shot!"

He said, "There was an awful lot of piss-offedness in that drive."

You won't find that word "piss-offedness" in any dictionary, but you wouldn't have to look it up, anyway. This gentleman's meaning was abundantly clear.

There are over 500,000 real words in the latest version of the Oxford English Dictionary, but for the humor writer, that may not be enough. If it isn't, feel free to manufacture one.

Earlier I used an example of the confusion over the word "why." I noted that when my wife and I talked about it we started to sound like Abbot and Costello. Since then I've used that phrase as a verb—"My wife and I start Abbott-and-Costelloizing." It probably won't make the next edition of the *OED*, but it serves my purposes from time to time.

Here are some examples of newly-coined words and phrases:

It was difficult discussing anything with this man. Any-

time I made a profound point, he said, "Balderdash." I'd make another pertinent argument. He'd say, "Balderdash." The man was a balderdashophile.

> I said to my spouse, "Uh-oh."
> She said, "What's that supposed to mean?"
> I said, "Well, roughly translated, it's an expression of uh-ohness."

> During our camping trip, my son insisted that we go bird watching. I know nothing about birds or bird watching, but I went along because he wanted it so badly. We didn't do badly. In less that two hours, we spotted two robins, and twenty-four non-robins.

Using words in a contradictory context: We use words to convey the thought we want to convey. Sometimes, though, a humor writer can employ them to convey exactly what that writer doesn't want to convey. For example:

> My wife came into the room, proudly wearing her brand new dress.
> She said, "How does it look?"
> I thought it looked terrible, so I told her so. "It looks great," I said.

> My wife's brother has been staying with us for some time now. He does absolutely nothing around the house and absolutely nothing outside of the house. I wish he would learn a trade so we would at least know what kind of work he's out of.

Using words out of context: One snippet I remember from reading humorous articles as a youngster—and I'll never be able to tell you who wrote it nor in which article—used words so deliciously inappropriately. The quote read:

> "Shut up," he explained.

What a wonderful example of words used out of context. You don't *explain* to someone that they should "shut up."

Here's another example that I wrote, obviously remembering the piece I read so many years before:

> **My wife insisted that I should clean out the garage this morning.**
> **"OK," I protested.**

Recalling again Shakespeare's admonition that brevity is the soul of wit, you don't get much briefer than a clever use of this device...and it can pack in the humor when used wisely.

Play back on previously used phrasing: Sometimes a humor writer can generate some fun by doing variations on sentence structures that were previously used in the article. Here's an example from an article I wrote about going shopping with my wife to find some decorative hanging that would fill an empty spot on our wall:

> **In one of the stores I saw a painting that I liked. It seemed to be around the right dimensions for our trouble spot. I said to my wife, "Do you like this?"**
>
> **"No." She said just the one word, "no," but the tone in which she said it implied: Please don't try to help me. This is a very agitating decorating question. I don't have time to educate you on the finer points of color, space, and aesthetics. I'd rather you amuse yourself reading wall plaques or T-shirts that have witty sayings on them. Thank you.**
>
> **I said, "Oh." I said just the one word, "oh," but the tone in which I said it implied: Oh.**

Changes in expected phrasing: Going back to the idea that humor is largely based on the element of surprise, this idea surprises the reader by implying a certain sequence of words or phrases, then changing it...usually at the end.

For instance, you might be enumerating reasons for something or other. "One—they're too expensive. Two—they're hard to find. And C—..." 1—2—C?

Dave Barry uses this device often in his wonderfully funny columns. He'll lead you to expect a certain wording, but the last item in his sequence will be outlandish, bizarre...and funny. Look for it in some of his columns.

Here are some other examples:

> **Our host can only play two songs on the banjo. One is "Has Anybody Seen My Gal," and the other one isn't.**

> **My office colleague only had three speeds—slow, slower, and notify the pallbearers.**

Play with modifiers: Modifiers play a big role in humor writing, too. They're the descriptive words that can paint a funny image or get across a witty idea. Here's an example from an article I did about my wife complaining that I never take her anywhere any more.

> **"You're becoming a real vegetable any more, do you know that?" my wife said to me without apparent cause.**
> **"Who, me?" I replied, making light of the situation by saying it with a sort of zucchini accent.**

In another piece, I had fun with an oft-changing modifier. This is from a piece about me getting lost while I was driving and my wife was doing the map-reading. We were looking for a Queen Creek Road, but I couldn't ask for directions once we got lost because I had trouble pronouncing this tongue-twister of a highway.

> **I said to my spouse/navigator, "Next we're looking for a sign that says 'Queen Kweek Woad."**

Notice my wife is now my "spouse/navigator." Later, in the article, though, when we've been lost awhile, she abdicates. Then a passage from the piece reads:

> **We drove some more, passing many of the same roads and byroads we had passed before. None of which were the elusive Queen Creek Road.**
>
> **My spouse/former navigator said, "I think you should stop and ask someone for directions."**

Later in the piece, I finally agree to ask for directions. But I want my wife to ask for the directions, so I must promote her once again. This portion reads:

> **Since we seemed to be hopelessly lost and driving in circles, I relented and pulled into a service station.**
>
> **I said to my spouse/reinstated navigator, "Go ask the man for directions."**

Using convoluted sentences: This one you've probably seen or heard many times. It goes something like this:

> **I knew what he wanted to do, but I also knew that he knew that I knew what he wanted to do. However, I knew something that he didn't know. I didn't want him to know that I knew something that he didn't know so I pretended that I only knew what he knew. Did he know something that I didn't know? I don't know.**

Well, you get the idea.

Here's an excerpt from a piece that I once did about two skunks who were named "In and "Out."

> **Once upon a time there were these two skunks named "In" and "Out." At the time, Out was out; and In was in.**

The mother skunk called "In" and said, "In, where's Out?"

In said, "Out's out."

The mother skunk said, "In, I want you to go out and get Out and bring Out in.

Again, you get the idea how the rest of this piece would go.

All of the above devices are tricks that are available to you as a comedy writer. Use them whenever they can help add some fun to your writing. Create new ones whenever the muse inspires you.

Writing humor is conveying your funny thoughts and images to the reader. We must do that with, as Hamlet replied to Polonius, words, words, words. The more you can make words work in a funny way for you, the better your humorous writing will be.

Chapter Twenty-one

Adding Humor to Serious Articles

In writing humorous pieces, you certainly need a generous helping of humor. A sprinkling of comedy in an otherwise serious piece has several benefits.

First, it makes the article more readable. Serious writing can be wearying for the reader. I know I often read through long articles in the morning newspaper. I should say, I try to read through them. Many times, I get only a fraction of the way through the piece and I say to myself, "Why am I reading this?" I stop reading.

A bit of humor along the way can be a nice "rest stop" for the reader and also a reward for persevering.

I can only judge other readers' reactions by my own because I can't sit and watch people read magazine or newspaper articles. However, I have evaluated audiences as they listen to speakers. As an observer I can usually tell when an audience is losing interest. The lecturer may be a learned expert but the audience tires of listening. When a speaker throws in a bit of whimsy, though, I can see the audience perk up. They've just been offered a little reward and they respond to it. Besides, they enjoyed that little aside so they now pay better attention because they don't want to miss any others.

Also, a judicious use of humor adds credibility to the writer of serious articles. It shows that the writer has perspective on his subject. Yes, it's an important topic, but the author can still find a little fun in it. It shows that the writer is taking the subject matter seriously, but not *too seriously.*

Most important, humor can be used to reinforce the most important elements in your article. Abraham Lincoln frequently used humor in his speeches and in his writing. In fact, he was often criticized by other politicians for trivializing whatever subject he was discussing. Lincoln didn't agree. He said about his humor, "I do not seek applause...nor to amuse the people. I want to convince them." Lincoln explained, "I often avoid a long and useless discussion by others or a laborious explanation on my own part by a short story that illustrates my point of view."

Good humor is short, concise, and to the point. It also should be very clear. People have to understand the point of the joke to laugh at it. Humor can express your point of view quickly, powerfully, and help make it readily understood. That makes for a powerful, effective piece of writing.

> "Humor can express your point of view quickly, powerfully, and help make it readily understood. That makes for a powerful, effective piece of writing."

Humor helps your message in another way, too. It helps the readers remember the most striking items in your article. Most memory aids instruct people to form wacky, bizarre pictures in their minds. The more outlandish the image is, the easier it will be for you to retain the concept.

For example, if you want to remember the number 345, you might use rhyming words like "tree," "door," and "hive." You imagine a huge tree with a trunk so large, that there is a bright red door in it. When you open the door, there's a giant beehive and the bees start attacking you. Now you should retain that picture and remember the number 345. Why? Because 345 is lifeless, it's unexciting. But a huge tree with a red door with a large beehive full of angry bees behind it? That's action. It's exciting. It's memorable.

Images are graphic and they seem to stay in our minds longer and are easier to recall. Humor is usually graphic, too. It generally conjures up an image in our minds. It will usually be easier for the readers to remember the funny images than the series of facts and figures that your article presents.

I can offer an example that affected me a long time ago. It was so long ago, in fact, that I can't give you a source because I can't remember it and would never be able to find it again. It was probably a self-help book making the point that to achieve any goal we must work hard and persevere. I'd probably read the same advice hundreds of times, but this one made an impression. Why? Because it was reinforced with a bit of humor. The author told about being on a trip of some kind with his young son. The boy spotted an inviting hill and wanted to climb to the top of it. The climb wasn't that inviting to the author. He explained to his son that it was a long way up that trail. It would be a rough, exhausting hike, and the father said that there was really no reason to expend that much energy. The boy said, "Unless being on the top of that hill is where you really want to be."

Through the years, I still think of that quote whenever I'm faced with a daunting, uninspiring task. That's how powerful and memorable you can make your message when you support it with a bit of wit.

"But I'm not a joke writer or a humorist," you say. That's all right. You can still add a touch of levity to your piece. "How?" you ask.

My first suggestion would be with your attitude, your approach to the subject you're writing about. Don't take it or yourself too seriously. That doesn't minimize the impact of your topic; it simply means to put it in proper perspective. Sure, your article is about something important. You think so or you wouldn't have thought about writing it and querying an editor about it. The editor agrees with you or she wouldn't have given you the go-ahead to write a first draft. Readers expect it will have impact or they wouldn't want to read it. You're writing about something that should be written about. However, it's not *the most important subject in the world.*

Bertrand Russell once said, "One of the symptoms of an approaching nervous breakdown is the belief that one's work is terribly important." Take a more light-hearted approach to your writing, regardless of the topic, and you may be able to uncover some of the inherent humor in it.

That's the first area to search for humor to include in your article—the subject itself. I recently did some humorous material for a doctor who is speaking to women about heart attacks among women. The purpose of her presentation was to make women aware that cardiovascular problems are a reality for females and that women's symptoms are unique. Certainly, that's a meaningful subject. Yet, we could present it with a touch of humor while keeping the message intact.

This doctor said, "For a long time, a lot of doctors were unaware of a woman's unique heart attack symptoms. There's a good reason for that—because a lot of doctors are men."

This gets a pleasant chuckle from the audience, but it also makes several points. It tells the listeners that female symptoms are different from male symptoms, that many doctors overlook that, and that the female patients had better take an interest in their own treatment and make sure that their doctors treat them for their particular ailment.

In researching your topic, look for those ironies that may be exposed with humor.

Often humor is expressing a truth in a clever or convoluted way. I often recount the story of a shopping trip I went on with my mother when I was a lad of about four or five. I wasn't happy being dragged along for a boring tour of department stores looking at dishtowels and glassware or whatever Mom was shopping for. I was a misbehaving terror. Mom got so angry at me that she said, "The next time I take you shopping, I'm leaving you home."

Her message was clear. She was angry and I had better behave. And I did behave, but not because of Mom's admonition. I didn't really care if she ever took me shopping again or not. But the logic of her illogical statement confounded me so much that I was too busy trying to figure it out to spend any more time being naughty.

I remember one time passing by a tennis court where friends of mine were engaged in a tennis match. I didn't know the score so I wasn't aware that these folks were being badly beaten. As I walked by, I said to one of them, "How's it going? He shouted back, "We have them right where they want us." It was a pretty clever way of saying they were getting thrashed.

I once did an article about a politician campaigning for office. I wanted to convey the idea that this politician, we'll call him Joseph L. Blow, was flip-flopping on every issue under discussion. He would be for a certain issue on a certain day in a certain place, but against that same issue on a different day in a different place. I said in the piece, "There are two sides to every political argument. First there is Joe Blow's side of it, and then there is Joe Blow's other side of it."

One way to add a touch of humor to your serious writing is to make a meaningful point with a whimsical use of wording or phrasing.

Another way to bring humor to a weighty subject is to illustrate it with cute, quaint, or downright funny anecdotes. You can gather these from humor anthologies, magazines like *Reader's Digest*, or taking note of stories you hear from friends or that have been sent to you on the internet.

To illustrate, I remember once reading an article about making the most of the skills you have. The author told about a football coach who was berating one of his players in front of the entire team for lack of effort. He ended his tirade by saying, "If I was your size I'd be the heavyweight champion of the world." The lad said, "I have one question, Coach." Coach said, "What?" The player said, "How come you're not the bantam weight champion?"

Using an cute anecdeote should not be an offense to your originality as a writer because you're not claiming it as your own. You readily admit that it's a story you heard or read but that you feel is pertinent to your message. You feel the reader should enjoy it, too.

It should not be an offense to your creativity, either. You researched it and noted how it would be helpful in illustrating your message. That's part of creative writing.

Finally, you might get some humorists to help you add some whimsy to your piece. You can do that by gathering witty quotes that support your ideas. Many famous people have had many funny things to say about many different topics. These are powerful quotes. That's why they've been preserved for so long—because they're good

You can borrow material from legendary comedians.

> *"Money is better than poverty, if only for financial reasons."*
> **—Woody Allen**

> *"The secret of staying young is to live honestly, eat slowly, and lie about your age."*
> **—Lucille Ball**

Or you could use material from some of the newer comics.

"Have you ever noticed? Anyone going slower than you is an idiot and anyone going faster than you is a maniac."
—George Carlin

Or you might gather some useful sayings from another breed of comedian—the politician.

"The nice thing about being a celebrity is that if you bore people, they think it's their fault."
—Henry Kissinger

You might also borrow some witty sayings from great thinkers of the past.

"My advice to you is to get married. If you find a good wife, you'll be happy; if not, you'll become a philosopher."
—Socrates

"He was a great patriot, a humanitarian, a loyal friend; provided, of course, he really is dead."
—Voltaire

"You ask me if I keep a notebook to record my great ideas. I've only ever had the one."
—Albert Einstein

"She had lost the art of conversation but not, unfortunately, the power of speech."
—George Bernard Shaw

You might refer to some great literary geniuses.

"As yet, Bernard Shaw hasn't been prominent enough to have any enemies, but none of his friends like him."
—Oscar Wilde

Whatever your topic, someone somewhere said something pertinent and witty about it. Finding that quote and using it can enhance your serious article with a touch of quality humor.

Of course, if you're still worried about sacrificing originality and creativity, consider this quote:

> *"The secret of creativity is knowing how to hide your sources."*
> **—Albert Einstein (a fairly creative guy)**

Chapter Twenty-two

Marketing Your Material

Which came first, the chicken or the egg? Which came first, the professional humor writer or the sale? By definition, you're not a professional writer until you make a sale. However, your sales depend on your being professional. So be professional first in order to make the first sale. In addition, the more professional you are as a writer, the more writing you'll sell.

What does being professional mean?

Your first duty as a professional is to yourself and, by extension, to your craft. There is one sure shortcut to success in the writing field—in any endeavor, for that matter—and that is by being good at what you do and always getting better at what you do. Michael Jordan earned millions playing basketball. Why? Because he was very good at playing basketball. Sinatra earned fame and fortune as a saloon singer. Why? Because he was a terrific saloon singer. Quality always attracts success.

Consider Tiger Woods. He wins golf tournaments against more experienced pros, he gets big bucks for endorsements, he draws huge crowds wherever he plays. Woods deserves the adulation and the financial rewards because he has devoted himself to the game of golf since he was a toddler. He appeared on television displaying his golf swing when he was only three years old. He had a nifty swing as a youngster and he's gotten better since. His practice and dedication is paying off grandly for him now.

However, imagine that Tiger Woods had never heard of golf. He never heard of the sport. He just happened to pick up a club one day and discovered that he could hit the dimpled ball far and straight. He was a natural golfer.

Even accepting that bizarre scenario, Tiger Woods would still be a golfing phenomenon within months. That sort of talent could not be denied. Someone would notice him on a driving range hitting balls over 300 yards. Someone would invite him to play and notice that he's scoring lower than the pros. Someone would tell someone and this kid would be on the PGA tour enjoying the same success he is presently.

Admittedly, this is an unbelievable supposition, but the principle is not that unbelievable. Quality will be noticed and will be rewarded.

The reason Tiger Woods is a sensation is because he's a sensational golfer. He has honed his craft magnificently.

The professional writer, too, must devote time and energy to developing those skills that are needed to produce outstanding work. Other areas demand attention also—marketing, making important contacts, and the like—but none of these should be at the expense of developing your talent.

It's professional writing that makes a writer a professional. Write well and the sales and accolades will follow.

As a professional, present a professional appearance, too

When I was writing for a comedian and traveling with him, a promoter approached this comic and wanted to offer him an arrangement that he guaranteed would "make you a million dollars."

That's a promise that's hard to reject, so the comic agreed to a luncheon meeting with this entrepreneur. I was invited to sit in on this get-together. The promoter approached our table with his briefcase and we introduced ourselves all around. Then the promoter sat down, opened his briefcase, and began. He said, "Er...uh..."

The comedian turned to me and said, "Man's going to make me a million dollars and he starts out with 'Er...uh...?'"

The meeting was effectively over. The man's presentation was laughed off. The comic never made the promised million bucks. The entrepreneur's poor first impression did him in.

Professional writers, too, must present a strong professional appearance. Of course, most writers, don't get a chance to sit down with editors and begin with "Er...uh..." We deal through the mails, over the phone, or via e-mail. Nevertheless, we still should present a professional image.

We do that with neat and knowledgeable documents.

Knowledgeable means that you should know how to write a suitable query letter, proposal, first draft, whatever. You should know what format they should be in, what fonts are preferred, what length is traditional, and so on.

> **"As a writer, your document represents you. If you aren't professional in preparing it, the buyer has to assume that you won't be professional in executing your assignment."**

I've rarely edited material for magazines, but as a television producer I read hundreds of audition scripts. It was a massive task just to read through all the teleplays that were submitted. Consequently, producers look for ways to shorten the ordeal. We did that by finding something in the script that would give us cause to reject it without reading further. If we opened a script that was in the wrong format, we'd toss it into the "reject" bin immediately. It might have been a great story with wonderful character development and hilarious joke lines throughout, but it would have gone unread. The wrong format labeled it amateurish. The writer's carelessness condemned it.

The copy should also be neat, clean, and relatively error free. A typo here or there and a questionable comma or two is not critical. A sloppy, careless manuscript very well could be.

Again, as a producer, I've received manuscripts that were handwritten. I told the author that handwritten documents were not acceptable.

He said, "I don't know how to type."

I said, "There are typists in town who will prepare your manuscript in a professional format."

He said, "I can't afford that."

I didn't say it but I thought, then you'll never be able to afford to be a writer.

As a writer, your document represents you. If you aren't professional in preparing it, the buyer has to assume that you won't be professional in executing your assignment. You won't get that many assignments.

Clean, neat, well-prepared manuscripts are important because of the image they project. Have you ever noticed that you see very few Rolls Royces on the road with crumpled fenders, doors painted a different color than the rest of the body, or red paper taped over a broken tail light? They're the best cars on the road and the owners care for them. They're usually clean and flawless.

That same care expressed in a manuscript shows that you're proud of your writing and confident with it. You're showing that you believe your product is the best available. You're announcing that yours is the Rolls Royce of manuscripts.

It influences buyers.

A professional follows instructions. I remember once being at a restaurant and I overheard the exchange at a table next to me. The waiter brought food that was not ordered.

The customer said, "I didn't order the halibut. I ordered the filet mignon."

The waiter checked and agreed that person had indeed ordered the steak. Nevertheless, he said, "Couldn't you just eat the halibut? It's very good."

If that diner wanted the halibut, she would have ordered the halibut. She ordered the filet mignon and she wanted to eat the filet mignon.

Sometimes we writers behave like that waiter. "I know you wanted an 800-word humorous piece, but wouldn't you really rather have this 3,600-word essay that I've written on the same subject? It's really very good."

If the editor wanted 3,600 words, she would have asked for 3,600 words. She asked for 800 words, and she has every right to expect, from a professional, 800 words.

Follow the instructions. If sometimes you do feel a change is warranted and beneficial, at least call the buyer to find out if it's O.K. to make that change. If you get that approval, go ahead and change away. If you don't get a go-ahead, don't.

A professional writer delivers what he or she promises to deliver. I recall one episode that astounded and confused me in dealing with writers. At a pitch session, a team of writers presented a proposal which my coproducer and I bought. The story was one that we hadn't used yet, and it seemed to have a certain intrigue to it. We worked on a few details and noted some changes, then sent the writers off to come up with a full outline. We congratulated them. They had a sale.

A week or two later, they returned for another meeting with an outline that was nothing at all like the story we had worked on with them and bought. It was an entirely different story. It was disjointed and not one that we wanted to do.

"Where's the story we discussed at the last meeting?" we asked.

"This one's much better," they said.

Well, it wasn't, but even if it was, it wasn't the one we bought. Their new story could have been one that was similar to one we already had in the works, or it could have been one that was not the type of story we wanted to tell. There might have been a hundred reasons we didn't want this new story.

We rejected it outright and asked them to come back with an outline of the story that we originally agreed to.

They came in a week or two later with still another completely different tale. We withdrew the offer and they lost the sale.

As a professional writer, you have an obligation to your client to deliver what the client wants and expects. You have an agreement with that buyer and as a professional you should live up to your end of that agreement.

If you have a new and better idea later, that's fine, but you have to resell that idea to the client.

It's as if you went to an appliance store and paid $800 dollars for a refrigerator. Then the delivery truck pulls up to your door and delivers an $800 electric stove. "It's the same price," the store owner says. "What's the difference?"

Well, there is a difference and you wouldn't be happy with it. The editor may not be happy when you change the product you deliver, either.

Now let's talk about some specific suggestions for submitting and selling humorous pieces.

1) This one I know you've heard before. It hardly bears repeating, but I'll repeat it anyway—know your market. This is really Basic Writing 101, however it still applies to writing humorous articles. Study the magazines that you want to submit to. Know what sort of articles they publish and what slant those articles take.

Again, this is a mark of professionalism. Editors don't enjoy receiving pieces that are obviously wrong for their publication. It not only uses up some of their valuable time, but it annoys them. Often they're offended that this writer has such a glaring ignorance of what they publish. They like to feel that their publication is well-known and well-read. When they get a manuscript that screams, "I don't know anything about your magazine," they're rightly bruised.

Now this doesn't mean that you can't be innovative. You needn't be tied down to *exactly* what's in the periodical today. The fact that they don't have a humor page in the magazine doesn't mean they can't have a humor page in a future issue. You might suggest a piece that knocks their socks off. Heck, it might become a regular. Certainly, you're free to suggest it.

Even in being daring, though, you should do it in keeping with their editorial policies. You still have an obligation to know something about that periodical and submit new proposals that are in keeping with those policies.

2) This suggestion goes against what you've probably heard before. It's anti-Basic Writing 101. Nevertheless, it applies for humorous writing. Tradition dictates that you submit a query before writing an article for a magazine. It saves you a lot of trouble. Why write an article if there's no buyer for it?

However, humorous pieces are the exception to the rule. The query in this case serves no real purpose. The effectiveness of humor is in the execution; not the basic premise. Besides, as I mentioned before, it's just as easy for you to write the piece as it is to compose a compelling query letter.

It takes the editor as much time to read the article as it would take to read the query letter. Also, it saves the editor time. He or she can accept or reject that piece then and there. With a query letter, they'd have to accept or reject the query…on condition. Then they'd have to again evaluate the final piece when it's written.

If you have an idea for a humorous article that you know from studying the periodical is something they might be interested in, write the article. Send it off. Cash the check.

3) This might be begging the question, but I'll beg the question anyway. Make it funny. Humorous articles are supposed to generate laughs, chuckles, inward smiles. Sometimes we can get so lost in our message that we forget the original purpose. Sometimes we can get carried away with style and technique and forget that we're writing and selling humor.

> "Make it funny. Humorous articles are supposed to generate laughs, chuckles, inward smiles."

There's nothing wrong with a momentous message. There's certainly nothing wrong with crisp, brilliant writing. However, if you're writing humor, keep it somewhat humorous.

Finally, a word about editors. They're important to professional writers because they're the ones who say "yea" or "nay." They're the ones who authorize the checks that you'll cash. They, for a free-lance writer, are the *customer*.

Editors are good people. They love writing and they love writers, they really do. Why do they love writers so? Because their job is to fill their respective publications with writing. That's easier for them if they have writers who can do the writing.

I used to travel with several editors of major magazines doing seminars at colleges around the country. These editors usually traveled great distances and prepared lectures for no financial recompense. They did it because they wanted to encourage writers and also to find a few good ones that they could add to their dependable stable.

Editors are busy people, though. I know because all of them mentioned that in their lectures. They have more to do each day than add or delete a few commas from the text or unmix a few mixed metaphors.

They have production meetings to attend, schedules to finalize, budgets to balance, revisions to make to their finalized schedules, adjustments to make to their previously balanced, now unbalanced, budgets so that they can afford to meet their re-revised finalized schedules... and a lot more that we can't even conceive of.

As a professional writer, you can help that editor by making her editing tasks easier by delivering quality material. Deliver it on time. Deliver it the way she wants it. Do all you can as a solid professional writer to allow the editor more time to devote to her schedules, budgets, and presentation at production meetings.

However, you are a busy person, too. Those same editors should have obligations to you, also. I remember when I attended these seminars, I would listen to the editors proclaim, "I answer every piece of mail that crosses my desk within four weeks." Of course, the time would vary, but each editor promised a response within a reasonable amount of time to any query or submission.

As an experiment once, I sent proposals to all of the editors. None responded in the promised time, and several never responded at all.

It seems unfair—in fact, downright unprofessional—to keep a writer waiting several months and then perhaps responding with an outright rejection. Admittedly, the editors are busy with the aforementioned schedules, budgets, and production meetings. However, writers are busy, too—with writing, writing, and writing.

> ● "As a professional writer, you can help that editor by making her editing tasks easier by delivering quality material. Deliver it on time. Deliver it the way she wants it."

Rejections are permissible. All of us writers expect them. But it is professional to expect them within a reasonable period.

To me, it is acceptable and professional to check on a submission after a certain period of time. If the editor's blurb in one of the market guides, such as *The American Directory of Writer's Guidelines* or *Writer's Market*, says they respond within four weeks, it's appropriate to check on that submission. If you get no response, then send it off to other markets.

After all, being a professional means making money from your writing. You can't make any money from a piece that's sitting on an editor's desk.

PART IV

Write

Chapter Twenty-three

Your Assignment

My assignment is done. I've written this book and passed along a few of the tips I've learned about writing humor over the years, along with some stories of the fun I've had along the way. I hope these chapters have encouraged and inspired you...and convinced you that you can write funny.

Your assignment now is to write and sell some hilarious articles.

As Bob Hope's head writer for many years, one of my duties was to pass on the assignments to the other writers. We called them "NAFT's." When Hope wanted some gags, he'd call the writers and say, "I need a few things on..." hence, the acronym.

I'm going to pass this assignment on to you with the same words I used when I gave the topics to all the writers I worked with—"Have fun with it."

Index

Gene Perret (left) with Bob Hope on a USO flight.

About the Author

Gene Perret has been a comedy writer since the early 1960s, working for comedians such as Slappy White and Phyllis Diller. He's been a television comedy writer and producer since 1968. The Beautiful Phyllis Diller Show was his first television staff assignment. Gene has also worked as a writer on:

"The Jim Nabors Show"
"Laugh-In"
"The New Bill Cosby Show"
"The Helen Reddy Show"
"The Carol Burnett Show"
"Mama's Family"
…and others

He was a head-writer/producer on:
"Welcome Back, Kotter"
"Three's Company"
"The Tim Conway Show"

And wrote episodes for:
"All in the Family"
"Joe and Sons"
"What's Happening!!"
"Gimme a Break"
"Love, American Style"
...and others.

Gene has also worked on Bob Hope's writing staff since 1969, many of those years as Hope's head writer. In this capacity Gene wrote for all of Bob's personal appearances and TV specials. Gene was the only writer to travel with the Bob Hope troupe to the war zones of Beirut, the Persian Gulf, Saudi Arabia, and on a peace time military jaunt around the world that featured stops at the Berlin Wall and in Moscow.

As a television writer, Perret has been nominated for seven Emmy nominations, including one for original music, and two Writer's Guild Award nominations. He has captured three Emmy awards and one Writer's Guild Award.

Gene has also written over thirty books on or about comedy, including the popular guide for comedy writers and performers *Comedy Writing Step by Step*.

Presently, Gene Perret writes a twice-monthly humor column for *Arizona Highways*. He has also written articles for *Reader's Digest*, *Good Housekeeping*, *McCall's*, *Parents*, *Toastmaster*, *The Writer's Digest*, and others.

. . . other great Quill Driver books on writing & publishing!

The ABCs of
Writing for Children

**114 Children's Authors and Illustrators Talk About the
Art, the Business, the Craft & the Life of Writing
Children's Literature**

—*by Elizabeth Koehler-Pentacoff*

A Writer's Digest Book Club Selection!

In The ABCs of Writing for Children *you'll learn the
many 'do's and don'ts' for creating children's books. You'll see
that what works for one author may not work for the next.*

66 ...a thorough, complete, entertaining guide to writing for
children—more alpha to omega than *ABCs*. I wish there was such a
volume for every aspect of my life! 99

—Karen Cushman, author of *Catherine, Called Birdy*

$14.95 ($22.95 *Canada*)

• ISBN 1-884956-28-9

DRAWING FROM PERSONAL EXPERIENCE
TO CREATE FEATURES YOU CAN PUBLISH

*Lifewriting is people-centered nonfiction writing. Not just
autobiographical or biographical, lifewriting encompasses a broad
range of personal-experience narratives. Lifewriting can be
serious, humorous or both. It can include any kind of subject
matter because people will always be at the heart of any
lifewriting endeavor. Fred D. White Ph.D., author of four
textbooks on writing, walks the reader through the lifewriting
process, from research to composition to revision to marketing.*

$14.95 ($22.95 *Canada*)

• ISBN 1-884956-33-5

Feminine Wiles
**Creative Techniques for Writing
Women's Feature Stories That *Sell***

—*by Donna Elizabeth Boetig*

Both titles are Writer's Digest Book Club Selections!

From *Feminine Wiles*: ...commit yourself. You are going to write
stories of women's struggles and joys. You are going to discover
information that changes the lives of readers. You are going to
predict trends and you may even create a few of your own. You
are going to look out into the world to see what's happening and
take what you find deep within yourself to figure out what it all
means—for you, and your readers.

66 More valuable than a dozen writer's workshops or journalism
courses. If you're interested in developing a successful career as a
freelance writer for women's magazines, read *Feminine Wiles*—and
get to work. 99

— Jane Farrell, Senior Editor *McCall's*

Available at better brick and mortar bookstores, online bookstores, at
QuillDriverBooks.com or by calling toll-free 1-800-497-4909

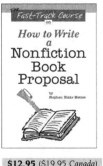
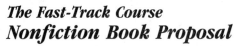